THE SPIRITUAL RESISTANCE OF RABBI LEO BAECK

The Spiritual Resistance of Rabbi Leo Baeck provides an overview of the life of Dr. Leo Baeck (1873–1956), a German-Jewish rabbi, theologian, historian and Holocaust survivor, from a psychoanalytic perspective.

Paul Marcus approaches Baeck's life and intellectual/theological contribution as it interfaces with a broadly defined psychoanalysis. This book describes and explains how Baeck maintained the rudiments of his autonomy, integration and humanity while remaining in Nazi Germany and while in the ghetto Theresienstadt, displaying astonishing courage, character, and goodness—a triumph of a civilized person amidst Nazi brutality. Marcus also considers psychic resilience and moral psychology and assesses contemporary criticisms of Baeck.

The Spiritual Resistance of Rabbi Leo Baeck will be of interest to academics and scholars of psychoanalytic studies, spirituality, Jewish studies and resistance. It will also appeal to psychoanalysts in training and in practice.

Paul Marcus is a training and supervisory analyst at the National Psychological Association for Psychoanalysis in New York City and co-chairperson of the discussion group Psychoanalysis and Spirituality at the American Psychoanalytic Association. He is the author of *Psychoanalysis and Toileting: Minding One's Business* and *Psychoanalysis and Wisdom: Encountering 'Ethics of the Fathers'* (Routledge).

Recently published Routledge titles by Paul Marcus

Psychoanalysis and Wisdom: Encountering 'Ethics of the Fathers' (2024)

Psychoanalysis and Toileting: Minding One's Business (2023)

Psychoanalysis as a Spiritual Discipline: In Dialogue with Martin Buber and Gabriel Marcel (2021)

Psychoanalysis, Classic Social Psychology and Moral Living: Let the Conversation Begin (2020)

The Psychoanalysis of Overcoming Suffering: Flourishing Despite Pain (2019)

The Psychoanalysis of Career Choice, Job Performance, and Satisfaction: How to Flourish in the Workplace (2017)

THE SPIRITUAL RESISTANCE OF RABBI LEO BAECK

Psychoanalysis and Religion

Paul Marcus

Routledge
Taylor & Francis Group
LONDON AND NEW YORK

Designed cover image: Courtesy of the Leo Baeck Institute, New York

First published 2025
by Routledge
4 Park Square, Milton Park, Abingdon, Oxon OX14 4RN

and by Routledge
605 Third Avenue, New York, NY 10158

Routledge is an imprint of the Taylor & Francis Group, an informa business

British Library Cataloguing-in-Publication Data
A catalogue record for this book is available from the British Library

ISBN: 9781032877594 (hbk)
ISBN: 9781032877600 (pbk)
ISBN: 9781003534327 (ebk)

DOI: 10.4324/9781003534327

Typeset in Times New Roman
by codeMantra

For Abey who is beginning his life and to
my dear friend Steven A. Luel who died of cancer
on September 1, 2024

CONTENTS

Acknowledgments *ix*

1 Introduction 1

2 Spiritual Resistance in Nazi Germany 12

3 Spiritual Resistance in Theresienstadt 40

4 Religious Consciousness and Theological Reflections 66

5 Implications for Psychoanalysis 80

References *95*
Index *103*

ACKNOWLEDGMENTS

I would like to thank Frank Mecklenburg, Director of Research, Leo Baeck Institute in New York for his helpful comments about my project and Professor Michael A. Meyer, Baeck's biographer, for his generous time in discussing the life and work of Leo Baeck and for reading an earlier version of the manuscript. Thanks also go to my wife, Irene, a child and adult psychoanalyst for her helpful comments on the manuscript. I am also grateful to Michael Eigen and Lawrence H. Schiffman for their promotional endorsements of my book. Finally, thanks to editor Susannah Frearson for her support of my writing project and to Saloni Singhania, her editorial assistant. I alone am responsible for what is written in this book.

"The greatness of the human soul is its power of resistance"
Rabbi Dr. Leo Baeck

1

INTRODUCTION

As a psychoanalyst I have often been troubled by what Freud wrote in letters to American neurologist James Jackson Putnam, "That psychoanalysis has not made analysts themselves better, nobler, or of stronger character remains a disappointment for me. Perhaps I was wrong to expect it" (Hale, 1971, pp. 163–164). Indeed, the aforementioned is in sync with Freud's overall outlook on the human condition, "The unworthiness of human beings, including the analyst, always impressed me deeply, but why should analyzed men and women in fact be better. Analysis makes for integration but does not itself make for goodness" (Hale, 1971, p. 188). While goodness is an extremely complex notion, I roughly define it drawing from philosopher Emmanuel Levinas: "Goodness consists in taking up a position being such that the Other counts more than myself" (1969, p. 247).

Dr. Leo Baeck (1873–1956), a German-Jewish rabbi, theologian, historian and Holocaust survivor, lived his life in a manner that was the opposite of Freud's above characterization: He personified nobility of spirit, strong character and goodness (Meyer, 2021). Baeck was described by German Professor D. Johannes Herrmann as a great man, exemplifying "a pure and mature intellectuality . . . join[ed] with a pure and unlimited goodness" (Friedlander, 1968, p. 265). The prominent philosopher Walter Kaufmann described Baeck as a "saintly man" (Kaufmann, 1981a [1958], p. 3) while Susannah Heschel (2021) described him as "a figure of enormous dignity and decorum," "a figure of noble bearing," "a moral hero" (n.p.).

Baeck, for instance, bravely remained in Germany as the spiritual leader of the German Jewish community, he was arrested five times by the Gestapo – allegedly to "soften him up" (Meyer, 2021, p. 135), and he refused numerous offers to immigrate to the U.K. and U.S.[1] He was deported to the Nazi ghetto Theresienstadt[2] (number 187894) in 1943, where he lectured from memory on Plato and Kant (and other philosophers and subjects),[3] and supported and comforted fellow inmates

DOI: 10.4324/9781003534327-1

(Jews and non-Jews). One Catholic inmate noted that Baeck "derived no benefits from his position as did some of the other leaders" (Baker, 1978, p. 302). Said Baeck after the war, "Ours is the responsibility for all the peoples of the world" (Feller, 2024, p. 134). Indeed, a number of Christian ghetto inmates said, "There was something about the man that recalled a prince of the church" (Baker, 1978, p. 2). Baeck's narcissism was highly modulated, for example, he never used the singular pronoun 'I', nor spoke in the first person in his preaching and writing (Baker, 1978, p. 48).[4] Baeck believed that "a sermon is not to be delivered. It is the person who must deliver himself. . . . The greatest message one can preach is one's life" (Pasachoff, 1992, p. 159).

This book describes and explains how Baeck maintained the rudiments of his autonomy, integration and humanity while remaining in Nazi Germany and while in Theresienstadt, displaying astonishing courage and character, a triumph of a civilized person amidst Nazi brutality (Baker, 1978).[5] Baeck's narrative of self-identity will in part be unpacked by drawing from the insights of Holocaust survivors Bruno Bettelheim, Primo Levi, Jean Améry, Viktor E. Frankl, Elie Wiesel, Anna Pawelczyńska and others (Marcus, 1999).[6] My hope is that by understanding Baeck's outlook and behavior, for example, his strongly felt, flexibly and creatively applied, transcendent-pointing moral beliefs and values (the transcendental impulse as a motive force), psychoanalysis as a discipline can begin to integrate these "findings" into its theory of human behavior, and thereby deepen and widen its practice as an art of living a good or flourishing life (henceforth, the good life). For as Freud noted, psychoanalysis can be a useful tool for assisting us to comprehend what he called the "riddles of the world in which we live" (1927, p. 253), "a key to the explanation of human phenomena in general (and not only pathological symptoms)" as Chasseguet-Smirgel emphasized (1984, p. 120). Likewise, Fryer (2004) noted, that "psychoanalysis is at its core a reading of how we live in the world, of our struggles with our past as it shapes our present and future" (p. 26). By better understanding Baeck's personal resiliency (he was relatively unchanged and unbroken), perhaps psychoanalysis can gain useful psychological and moral insights into unusual and praiseworthy individual behavior that can enrich our theoretical discipline and practically help our patients (e.g., Baeck was an outstanding example of "resistance of the human intellect and human spirit" (Friedlander, 1995, p. ix)). And philosopher Esther Seidel noted, Baeck "was a prime example of how a human being, when faced with evil and death, could conduct himself with dignity and self-respect, and yet remain fully responsible for his fellow men" (Seidel, 1995, p. 111). As Baeck said after the war,

> It almost appears to me like a miracle how I have gone through everything, when I think how I have passed on a close fringe in the hard years, always, as if in the last minute, protected and guarded. For twenty-eight long months, my longing dream was to see once again a meadow, a field, or even a wood; to go once again one day to bed without being hungry; it was a great dream to be once

> again among the living and not among the dying—sometimes, day after day, a hundred of the men would die in the camp. I cannot speak about the even greater misery there and about the greater longing.

Baeck may have also felt some survivor guilt:

> Before me so often appears the shadows, the shadows of those who died and the shadows of those who led them to their deaths. . . . It is difficult to become totally reestablished after a difficult time, and perhaps the healing process sometimes lasts as long as the illness.
>
> *(Baker, 1978, pp. 320–321)*

Discerning Baeck's resiliency is a challenging, though not impossible exercise because according to philosopher Emil L. Fackenheim, himself one of Baeck's students in Berlin and a survivor of Sachsenhausen, Baeck "took the horrors he knew, silently, to his grave" (Fackenheim, 2001, p. 56). Indeed, according to his biographer, "a personal letter indicates that he had difficulty expressing his emotions" (Meyer, 2021, p. 74).[7] Said Baeck, "One day, I saw myself exposed, for the first time in my life, to the emotional outburst of a stranger, which I had great difficulty in restraining and redirecting into objective channels" (Brann, 1963, p. 138). Baeck exhibited "consummate control . . . over his emotions" (Friedlander, 1968, p. 206), perhaps a way of being that was typical of the German national character of the time (i.e., the Professor).

As one of the seminal explicators of Baeck, Rabbi/teacher Albert Friedlander noted (1968), Baeck was also a leading liberal Jewish theologian,[8] and as a scholar he should be set alongside the compelling thought of the great 20th-century Jewish religious philosophers, his friends Martin Buber (1878–1965), Franz Rosenzweig (1886–1929), and Abraham Joshua Heschel (1907–1972), who had studied under Baeck (Meyer, 2021). As Homolka noted, "Baeck can be considered" one of "the great theologian[s] of modern Jewish thought" (1995, p. 46). Baeck also integrated some important ideas from the neo-Kantian philosopher Hermann Cohen such as his emphasis on ethics and the messianic horizon.[9] In other words, Baeck, a religious stoic, a metaphysical poet, integrated the traditions of Eastern Jews with the intellectuality of western scholarship (Baker, 1978).[10] Moreover, the "full implications" of Baeck's theology "emerge only when the work is placed into the life of the author" (Friedlander, 2024, n.p.). That is, Baeck amalgamated what he believed in, his rigorous and pristine moral values, with how he lived his everyday life (i.e., he practiced what he preached). His profound faith in the Almighty implied his inescapable acceptance of moral obligation in all domains of his life (Meyer, 2021). As Baeck noted about the state of the world during the Cold War, "without religion and faith to inspire peace, peace cannot be achieved," further adding that it was religion that kept him, and his fellow inmates in Theresienstadt, "spiritually healthy" (Feller, 2024, pp. 177–178).[11] "Faith," for Baeck "is performing His will"

(1964 [1955], p. 25). And again, following Rabbi Simlai, a third-century Talmudic scholar, Baeck quoted that the synopsis of all of the commandments was that "the righteous shall live by faith" (1964 [1955], p. 392). That is, for Baeck, Judaism was a resource for optimism,[12] spiritual energy and steadfastness as he confronted adversity (Feller, 2024).[13] Said Baeck, "One must live to survive, live as if there will be a tomorrow" (Baker, 1978, p. 257).

Thus, this book also aims to contribute to deepening and expanding the psychoanalytic understanding of religion. In particular, how Baeck's theology and religious practices, for example his "religion of polarity" with its dialectical movement between the "mystery" of the divine presence in life (e.g., God is hidden and unfathomable)[14] and the "commandment" (e.g., goodness, devotion, selflessness, faith and reconciliation) of the ethical imperative that comes to a person in an encounter with God (Friedlander, 1968, 2024) (that "comes to mind" as Levinas described it), can help a person maintain his autonomy, integration and humanity amidst the extreme situation. Thus, this book will discuss in what ways religion, without being moralistic or indoctrinating, can contribute to making psychoanalysis a robust "spiritual discipline" (Marcus, 2021), such as viewing God as something like a self-sustaining universal matrix (Jones, 1991). It was Ludwig Binswanger (1963) who famously pointed out to Freud that a therapeutic failure they were conversing about could "only be understood as the result of something which could be called a deficiency of spirit" (p. 1). Binswanger was surprised when Freud agreed, asserting, "Yes, spirit is everything". Freud further elaborated, "Man has always known he possessed spirit: I had to show him there is such a thing as instinct" (Binswanger, 1963). Said Baeck, "Now the great miracle fulfills itself within the spirit: men discover their true selves in selflessness, so that they begin to understand themselves" (1964 [1955], p. 400).

Who was Leo Baeck?

A brief summary of the life of Baeck is as follows:[15]

Leo Baeck was born May 23, 1873, in what was then Prussia, and died in London on November 2, 1956 (aged 83). He was the son of the local rabbi (a notable scholar), one of eleven children (the only one who became a rabbi).[16] Baeck first pursued his higher education in Breslau (University of Breslau) and the conservative Jewish Theological Seminary. Mainly in order to study with the illustrious religion scholar Wilhelm Dilthey, Baeck transferred to Berlin (University of Berlin), where he earned a doctorate in 1895. His dissertation was on Spinoza. Two years later, he was ordained as a rabbi at the Hochschule für die Wissenschaft des Judentums, a leading institution of liberal Judaism in Berlin. Baeck then held pulpits in Oppeln (Silesia) and Düsseldorf, and in 1912 he was called to Berlin where, with the exception of being a chaplain during the First World War for about four years,[17] he remained until his deportation to Theresienstadt in 1943 (he was age 69).[18]

During his years in Berlin, Baeck assumed a number of progressively influential positions in his community. In 1913 he joined the faculty of the Hochschule as a docent of Midrash (early rabbinic sermons) and homiletics (the art of preaching). In 1922 he became chairman of the national association of German rabbis, and in 1925 he assumed the presidency of the B'nai B'rith, a fraternal network, in Germany (Wertheimer, 1987, n.p.). In 1937, Baeck's beloved wife Natalie, whom he had married in 1899, died from a stroke (probably exacerbated by the Nazi brutality she lived under) when he was 63 (he was devastated); their daughter Ruth, born in 1900, immigrated with her husband and daughter to England after *Kristallnacht* (the "Night of Broken Glass," also known as the November pogrom, November 9 to November 10, 1938). Baeck did not see his daughter, son-in-law and granddaughter for about six years.

When Hitler became the German Chancellor, it was Baeck who had the foresight to declare that "the thousand-year" history of German Jewry had come to an end (Meyer, 2021, p. 92). Baeck was the first choice by the founders to lead the *Reichsvertretung der Deutschen Juden* [National Representation of Jews in Germany],[19] an organization that made the most effective attempt in German-Jewish history to integrate Jewish defense, welfare, and cultural activities on a national scale. As president of this representative body, he devoted himself to defending the rights of Jews in Germany, enabling their emigration, and bolstering the morale of those still remaining in Nazi Germany. A noteworthy example of the last effort was a special prayer composed by Baeck for public recitation on the Day of Atonement (Yom Kippur) in 1935, which included a defiant rejection of Nazi slanders: "In indignation and abhorrence, we express our contempt for the lies concerning us and the defamation of our religion and its testimonies" (Wertheimer, 1987, n.p.). Baeck persisted in his refusal to flee Germany until every Jew had been rescued. He would stay in Germany "so long as even a minyan [a prayer quorum of ten men] was left" (Fackenheim, 2001, p. 53). In fact, Baeck brought "a trainload of children abroad and returned to enter the concentration camp with his people" as late as 1939 (Friedlander, 1968, p. 41). Baeck continued to head the national body of German Jews after it was forcibly reorganized by the government into a council that was answerable to the Nazis.[20] In January 1943, Baeck was deported along with other elderly German Jews to Theresienstadt (one of his initial jobs was to pull a wagon containing refuse or scraps of bread, potatoes and other items through the ghetto (Meyer, 2021). According to Meyer (2021) Baeck used "the occasion to discuss Plato and Isaiah with a fellow wagon-pulling Jew," and by doing so he experienced the heavy physical labor as more tolerable (p. 150).[21]

In that "model" or "show piece camp" for "privileged Jews" (Baker, 1978, p. 282) Baeck served as honorary president of the ruling Jewish council and devoted his time to comforting and teaching his fellow inmates.[22] At Theresienstadt, Baeck's life was spared initially due to the fact that the ghetto authorities confused him with another man of the same sounding name (Rabbi Beck from Moravia) who had already perished (Baeck had an ironic face-to-face discussion with Adolf Eichmann about this).[23] On May 8, 1945, twenty-four hours before Baeck's planned execution, Theresienstadt was liberated by the Russian army.[24] When the ghetto was liberated, he still refused to leave his flock until he was sure of their safety (and he forbade survivors taking revenge on the Nazi guards by killing them). He refused an invitation to be one of the first to depart, referencing that he needed to assist other needy survivors, even though he retrospectively viewed his experiences at Theresienstadt as "years of horror," a "terrible ordeal" (Feller, 2024, p. 147). He felt it was "his duty" to remain (Fackenheim, 2001, p. 55).

Baeck was in the ghetto for two years and four months and witnessed the death of many prisoners by illness, starvation and despair (Baker, 1978).[25] He gave humanizing lectures by memory to the other prisoners, Jewish and non-Jewish, on philosophical and religious thinkers like Plato, Kant and Maimonides.[26] Said Baeck, "People in distress should be helped to expand their brains and to think of something other than the present" (Meyer, 2021, p. 158). He also cared for prisoners through many small acts of kindness. He was generally speaking, described as "gentle and kind" though he could be "combative" when necessary (Meyer, 2021, p. x). Said Baeck, "One can have a strong faith and pious experiences without being disturbed by slavery, torture, and public horrors" (1981a [1958], p. 214). This book in part, attempts to offer some possible explanations for this statement. Indeed, Baeck's theology has been called a "theology of suffering" (Friedlander, 1995, p. xxi), and included a "prophetic mysticism" in the sense of a visionary, trans-rational proximity to God. That is, for Baeck, true mysticism is prophecy, the prophetic mystic points toward the truths which lies beyond the earthly realm (Schweid, 1994, pp. 158, 155).

Baeck immigrated to London after the war in 1945 and lived with his daughter. Said Baeck, "After all the dread and the pain that had surrounded and accompanied me, here I was met with joys, the joys of everyday, of being with my children and [my granddaughter] Marianne" (Meyer, 2021, p. 167). While he reflected on his appalling experiences in anger, he did not dwell on them, rather he looked forward, even with a degree of hope, toward his future (Meyer, 2021, p. 166).

The last years of his life were devoted to work on behalf of the World Union for Progressive Judaism, teaching at the Hebrew Union College (the Reform rabbinical school in Cincinnati, Ohio), and organizing and assisting the survivors of German Jewry. In England, he served as president of the Council of Jews from Germany. And shortly before his death, Baeck helped found an international research institute for the study of central European Jewry that bears his name (the Leo Baeck Institute, with sites in London, New York and Jerusalem). Incidentally, Carl Jung met Baeck after the war "pleading that the rabbi have some understanding for" his "initial support for the Nazi regime" (Meyer, 2021, p. 168). Baeck listened to Jung's "lame excuse"[27] and as he appeared to be repentant, their relationship was restored (they had been acquaintances at the Keyserling School of Wisdom) (Meyer, 2021, pp. 168–169). Baeck believed that while he could personally forgive someone who had done him harm, he could not forgive on behalf of those who had suffered or been murdered. Only God can pass such judgment (Feller, 2024).

Baeck's writings reflect his lifelong efforts to defend his people and faith. By faith Baeck means "the fulfillment of man's relation to the covenant; it forms the unity and the steadiness which he gives his life" (1964 [1955], p. 24). He achieved early fame by refuting the anti-Jewish claims of Adolf von Harnack, a liberal Protestant theologian and church historian, who denigrated Judaism in his book *Das Wesen des Christentums* [The Essence of Christianity]. Harnack alleged that Judaism was overly legalistic and a negative tradition (Feller, 2024). Baeck's first book, a polemical work entitled *Vorlesungen über das Wesen des Judentums* [Lectures on the Essence of Judaism, 1905], continued this defense and confidently, though respectfully, alleged Judaism superior to Christianity,[28] a claim that gained Baeck significant attention as a defender of German Jewry. Utilizing the approach to religion developed by his mentor, German philosopher Wilhelm Dilthey, Baeck attempted to illuminate the underlying psychology of Judaism and comprehend the Jewish religion in its totality. Indeed, Baeck was "a psychologist of religion in the deep sense in which Dilthey understood the term as 'empathy'" (Homolka, 1995, p. 69).

In following essays and reworkings of his first book, *The Essence of Judaism*, Baeck clarified and honed the distinctions between Judaism and Christianity: the latter, he claimed, was a "romantic religion" that praised enthusiastically feeling, self-indulgence, dogma,[29] and passivity; Judaism, by contrast, was a "classical religion" infused mainly with ethical considerations, being-for-the-other, as Levinas says. In Judaism, Baeck saw a religion in which God's mystery and commandment exist as existential polarities. *Dieses Volk: Jüdische Existenz* [This People Israel: The Meaning of Jewish Existence], a book which was partly written in Theresienstadt and completed after he was liberated, explored the meaning of Jewish existence in historical context. Written during the blackest era of Jewish history, it is a work of optimism and hope that conveys Baeck's belief in the eternity of the Jewish people and their ongoing mission to bring ethical monotheism to the world. In defiant refusal of Nazi barbarism, Baeck affirmed the messianic role of the people Israel to be ever mindful of God's ethical command. According to Baker (1978), Baeck was initially not a Zionist, though he saw a role of a national consciousness in Zionism, there is some indication that he became more Zionist while an inmate in Theresienstadt (Baker, 1978) and during his last years when he visited Israel a few times and lectured at Hebrew University. Baeck was "an enthusiastic cultural Zionist" in the last decade of his life, saying, "There cannot be Jewish hope, spiritual, moral, messianic hope without embracing Israel" (Meyer, 2021, p. 190).

Defining Psychoanalysis

I conceptualize psychoanalysis as a form of life, a meaning-giving, affect-integrating, and action-guiding resource for individuals who can appropriate the life- and identity-defining narrative of psychoanalysis when they seek to understand, endure, and possibly gain some mastery of the problems that affect, if not assault, the human experience of love, work, faith, and suffering (e.g., conflict, anxiety, despair, loss and tragedy). As philosopher Pierre Hadot notes about ancient Greek philosophy, psychoanalysis can be understood as a "spiritual exercise," a tool for living life skillfully, more fully and wisely (1997, p. 83). The aim of a spiritual exercise is to foster a deep modification of an individual's way of "seeing and being," a decisive change in how one lives one's practical, everyday life. Michel Foucault (a student of Hadot's) also discussed spiritual exercises, calling them "technologies of the self": "an exercise of the self, by which one attempts to develop and transform oneself, and to attain a certain mode of being" (1989, p. 433). Most importantly, the objective of a spiritual exercise is "a total transformation of one's vision, life-style, and behavior" in the service of increased personal freedom and equipoise (Hadot, 1997, pp. 14, 83, 103) and, I would add, a less self-centric outlook and behavior. According to this view, as Levinas described "Jewish humanism" at its best, psychoanalysis is "a difficult wisdom concerned with truths that correlate to virtues" (Levinas, 1989, p. 275).

Psychoanalysis is a painful, deconstructive, demythologizing, and defamiliarizing process for acquiring greater self-awareness and self-understanding, especially of one's destructive unconscious emotional activity, one that transforms moral consciousness by expanding and deepening one's capacity to love. As Freud suggested, at least ideally, self-understanding leads to self-mastery, which leads to self-transcendence of one's impediments to being more other-directed, other-regarding, and other-serving (i.e., less crudely narcissistic and in other ways neurotically self-absorbed). In fact, Freud described psychoanalytic treatment as the "scientific cure by love" (McGuire, 1974, pp. 12–13). In this sense, psychoanalysis is animated by both the "love of wisdom" and the "wisdom of love," by Greek and Hebrew values (Levinas, 1981, p. 162), and is a powerful tool for the art of living a good life as one construes and fashions it.

Notes

1 Baeck was asked to teach at Oxford University and also officially invited to live in the U.S. in 1940, but declined both offers (Baker, 1978). It should be mentioned that in about 1941 "Baeck had reached the point of despair and may at least have been thinking about his own emigration," though rabbinic duty called and he remained in Nazi Germany (Meyer, 2021, p. 114).

2 Baeck referred to Theresienstadt as a concentration camp.

3 According to Meyer (2021), formal lecturing in Theresienstadt began six months before Baeck was incarcerated and continued until May 1945. There were about 2,430 lectures given by a variety of speakers and they were usually held at night in a crowded barracks. Baeck was a very well-received lecturer by other inmates (he lectured on about 38 topics, only one lecture survived). As Baeck said, "he had loved the light. But in Theresienstadt, light and life arrived only when darkness fell. 'There,' he concluded, 'I learned to love the dark'" (Meyer, 2021, p. 155). Baeck further elaborates: "I shall never forget these meetings . . . we would assemble in pitch darkness. To light a candle or even a match would have brought immediate disaster upon all of us. Nevertheless, in the midst

of all that darkness I sensed light. The faces of these Jews were illuminated by unearthly radiance, as one was talking to them about matters of the spirit and eternal questions, about God, about Jews and the world, about the eternity of Israel. I sensed a light in that darkness, the light of the Torah . . . I often contemplated my people . . . their faces I could not distinguish, but I saw great light" (Berkovits, 1979, p. 12).

4 This being said, Baeck sometimes preached "somewhat monotonously," if not too cerebrally. In fact, one of the Trustees of the Jewish Community of Berlin who heard him preach spoke of his sermons as "Baeck's private conversations with God," possibly suggesting inordinate self-absorption (Bamberger, 1958, p. 2). As Baker (1978) noted, Baeck was a "reticent person himself, not given to showing emotion, an intellectual whose sermons still appealed more to the head than to the heart," the content being better than the delivery (p. 50). As I have said, in Theresienstadt, his lectures to fellow inmates were extremely well-regarded, suggesting that the extreme context potentiated Baeck's delivery. (Also, by then, he had learned in Düsseldorf the art of public speaking (Meyer, 2024)).

5 Baeck gave the invocation at the U.S. House of Representatives on February 12, 1948, the anniversary of Abraham Lincoln's birth. As Meyer (2021) further says, "Baeck had long admired" Lincoln "for his integrity and courage" (p. 186).

6 Bruno Bettelheim was a concentration camp survivor, while the other survivors heretofore mentioned were death camp survivors. I will also be drawing from the work of sociologists Anthony Giddens, Zygmunt Bauman, Erving Goffman and Michel Foucault among other interdisciplinary scholars. The work of philosophers Martin Buber, Gabriel Marcel and Emmanuel Levinas will also be used to illuminate Baeck's life and intellectual contributions (Marcus, 2021, 2008).

7 Along these lines, Baeck acknowledged having "a bit of puritanism, a bit of asceticism" to his way of comporting himself, similar to other rabbis of his time as he noted (Friedlander, 1968, p. 17). In fact, Baeck wrote "The 'Law' [halacha] also insures that human life contains a touch of asceticism with which no religion can dispense. It has taught self-control, moderation, sobriety and liberty against license, thought as against impulse" (Baeck, 1958, p. 74). A later generation of rabbis like Joachim Prinz were steeped in Weimar culture (Meyer, 2024).

8 Liberal Judaism of the time was probably somewhere between Reform and Conservative Judaism.

9 Following Cohen, Baeck believed that "suffering is the price Jews must pay to carry out their messianic role in history" (Borowitz, 1983, p. 50). See Beiser (2018) for a very good intellectual biography of Cohen.

10 Baeck was fluent in Hebrew, Latin and Greek, as well as his native German. He also was able to converse in Russian and spoke English (Baker, 1978). Abraham Joshua Heschel, the great Jewish theologian affirmed that Baeck was "'the most educated man'" he had ever met" (Meyer 2021, p. 123). According to Brann, while a student in Breslau and Berlin, Baeck was asked why he did not designate time for recreation and relaxation, his reply: "Where could I find any finer recreation and spiritual pleasure than in the writings and meditations of great thinkers of the past" (Brann, 1963, p. 135). "An orderly mind" Baeck told his students, "is not a matter of intellect but of character" (Baker, 1978, p. 104).

11 Baeck, like Martin Buber, preferred the word "religiosity" rather than religion (Meyer, 2021, p. 78). Buber justified "religiosity against religion, the private practice of the I-Thou, over against institutional pieties" (Borowitz, 1983, p. 156). While Baeck was affiliated with liberal Judaism, he was "very much a traditionalist in his personal living habits"; "The rituals have a poetic quality and observing them gave a life a new sense of beauty" (Baker, 1978, pp. 114, 115). "Religion preserves this poetic power" (Baeck, 1948, p. 92).

12 As Baeck noted, "Perhaps a human being does not die until he no longer sees anything but the past and the present moment" (Baeck, 1966 [1947], p. xxv). Baeck's outlook throughout his ordeal of suffering was future oriented, an expression of what appears

to be his characterological optimism (aka dispositional optimism). Interestingly, Baeck developed Judaism as a "religion of optimism," suggesting that his religious outlook and personality development potentiated each other.

13 Religion of course, has its "dark" side, indeed much evil has been perpetrated in a variety of forms by devotees who claimed they were doing "God's work."

14 Early on in his scholarly career, Baeck rejected mysticism in line with the liberal perspective on Judaism (i.e., mysticism was viewed as irrational). Later on, after careful study, he began to regard mysticism favorably believing that it revealed deep religious truths (Feller, 2024). Said Baeck, "All mysticism is fundamentally the same, being born out of the universal human longing to travel the way to divinity, to be with its immediacy" (1964 [1955], p. 322). However, if we define a mystic as "One who wishes to transcend individuality by union with Deity," Baeck is no mystic (Borowitz, 1983, p. 144). As Meyer quotes Baeck: "In every person there is a secret remainder, which lies beyond calculation and analysis. What is decisive in a person's life is not mere rational consideration, not only the clear direction of ideas but rather what is mysterious—the anonymous remainder in every person. Innermost in every person dwells something that is hidden" (Meyer, 2021, p. 66). Indeed, this quoted passage could have been written by Freud.

15 I have liberally drawn from Wertheimer's (1987) review article in this section.

16 I have been unable to find additional details about Baeck's early life.

17 It has been alleged by Brann (1963) that "the total collapse of the German front brought about a chaotic situation for all in charge of military units and their immediate assistants, and it took all of Baeck's moral strength to avoid a serious nervous breakdown. He was hospitalized for a time in any army clinic, where he suffered from what we would today call a psychosomatic disorder, and fears were expressed in Berlin circles as to whether he would be able to take up his full rabbinical duties" (p. 141). Unfortunately, Brann does not give a reference for this allegation and it has not been referenced in either of the two biographies of Baeck (Baker, 1978; Meyer, 2021).

18 In general, older folks represented the "bottom layer" in the severely segmented inmate community of Theresienstadt. Assimilated, middle-class Czech Jews were the dominant group. Theresienstadt was "not very Jewish" (Hájková, 2020, pp. 1, 5).

19 Later it was forced to rename itself *der Juden in Deutschland*, that is, Jews in Germany (Meyer, 2024).

20 Baeck had to make some very tough moral decisions while the head of German Jewry and in Theresienstadt. These challenging moral decisions that constitute moral psychology will be discussed in Chapters 2 and 3.

21 Upon arrival in Theresienstadt, Baeck had also volunteered to supervise the ghetto's welfare program, visiting/comforting the sick and elderly in this role. At the age of 70, he was no longer compelled to do forced labor, this being the standard policy. He was aged 69 when he arrived in Theresienstadt (Pasachoff, 1992, p. 153).

22 Baeck did not use his council authority to give extra help to his family and friends, for example, his niece and nephew were deported to a death camp. He lost four sisters in Theresienstadt, three before he was deported and one while he was there. He also lost two brothers in a death camp as well as other extended family members. Baeck has given a different fact pattern with regards to how many sisters died in Theresienstadt and survived the war, some have alleged that Baeck confused the facts for self-serving reasons (Hájková, 2020). Of course, the fact that he was probably traumatized by his ordeal of suffering can contribute to memory distortions.

23 In other words, Baeck physically survived only by accident, not an uncommon account according to other survivors of the Holocaust.

24 "Of the approximately 140,000 Jews transferred to Theresienstadt, nearly 90,000 were deported to points further east and almost certain death. Roughly 33,000 died in Theresienstadt itself." (U.S. Holocaust Memorial Museum, 2024).

25 Dysentery was a major problem in the ghetto; Baeck fasted for three days in order to recover from it. Said Baeck, "We had two prisons in reality. One made by the Germans and one because of the typhus" (Baker, 1978, p. 5). In general, sanitation was markedly inadequate in Theresienstadt (Baker, 1978; Marcus, 2023). Baeck had lost 70 pounds in weight by the time he was liberated by the Russians on May 8, 1945. In addition, the Nazis displayed sadistic treatment regarding toileting as well as at other times during the inmates' ordeal.

26 Initially, the lectures were forbidden, but by 1943 they were tolerated by the Nazi rulers (Hájková, 2020).

27 These are Meyer's words.

28 According to Friedlander, Baeck believed that "Christianity" was "the daughter which the mother [Judaism] could never hate." In fact, says Friedlander, "Baeck loves Christianity" (1968, pp. 107, 111). Said Baeck, "The more Judaism understands itself, the more it will realize the greatness which is Christianity. The Christian church should never forget that for her there can be no Bible without the Jewish Bible" (Meyer, 2021, p. 197). Baeck, along with Martin Buber and Franz Rosenzweig were mainly responsible for opening the gates to interreligious dialogue (Homolka, 1995).

29 Baeck (1981b) defined dogma as "a doctrine backed up by authoritative power" (p. 46) something which he alleged Judaism did not have, other Jewish scholars have disagreed with him. Baeck believed that what distinguished Judaism from Christianity was the absence of dogmas.

2

SPIRITUAL RESISTANCE IN NAZI GERMANY

How did Baeck maintain the rudiments of his autonomy, integration and humanity, the basis of his goodness, while living in Nazi Germany? This involved a number of interrelated meaning-giving, affect-integrating, action-guiding processes which I will attempt to explicate and understand. However, before getting to the heart of this chapter, I want to briefly define the seven key terms that will act as the lynchpin of my organizing framework namely, spiritual resistance, autonomy, integration, humanity (aka "remaining human"), beliefs, values and the "extreme situation."[1]

Some Important Definitions

1) Spiritual resistance is clearly defined on the Yad Vashem website:

> In Holocaust terminology, 'spiritual resistance' refers to attempts by individuals to maintain their humanity and core values in spite of Nazi dehumanization and degradation. Such unarmed resistance came in many forms, religious and non-religious, cultural, and educational. It proved that physical survival was not the only decisive quality of a person and it certainly was not the only matter of importance even to people in the most dire conditions.[2]

Spiritual resistance then, is in part, the conscious and unconscious ways that an inmate sustained his self-esteem, self-continuity and self-coherence. Spirit, "is the ability to bind together, to unite, to reconcile, to bring peace" (Baeck, 1964 [1955], p. 210). "The individual gains his power from the spiritual, out of the fundamental realm in which will, feeling, and thinking are a unity or become one" (1964 [1955], p. 277). The aforementioned is especially important because for Baeck there was a direct confrontation between Nazism and Baeck, qua rabbi. That is, for Baeck

DOI: 10.4324/9781003534327-2

(and others) Nazi ideology was fundamentally not a political one, "but a nihilistic rebellion against all human values and a satanic defacing of the divine image of which man is the bearer on earth" (Berkovits, 1979, p. 81). In other words, Baeck waged a spiritual battle against a Nazi movement that grossly betrayed the spirit as he conceived it (Berkovits, 1979). Religious salvation was contingent on his own moral effort, God demanded He be served by a life of righteousness (Cohen, 1971).

2) Following the brilliant formulations of Bruno Bettelheim, by autonomy, I mean:

> Man's inner ability to govern himself, and with a conscientious search for meaning despite the realization that, as far as we know, there is no purpose in one's life. It is a concept that does not imply a revolt against authority qua authority, but rather a quiet acting out of inner conviction, not out of convenience or resentment, or because of external persuasion or controls.
>
> *(Bettelheim, 1960, pp. 84–85)*

Thus, "To act morally, is to act autonomously, not as a result of social pressure" (Williams, 1993, p. 8).[3]

It should be emphasized that for Bettelheim, autonomy does not mean that the individual has "free reign," since "all society depends for its existence and growth on a balance between individual self-assertion and the general welfare. If man's instincts were unchecked, society could not exist" (Bettelheim, 1960, pp. 84–85). The fact is that in Nazi society there was a lethal progression of anti-Jewish actions that Baeck had to contend with up until his incarceration in Theresienstadt, a transit camp located in Northwestern Czechslovakia, where things got much worse. For example, he was continually trying to balance the needs of his community, his flock, with the demands of the Nazi authorities, sometimes making very tough and controversial moral decisions as I will discuss later.

3) By integration, I am referring to a person who has attained an internal harmony between one's evolving personal strivings, one's beliefs and values and the changing demands of the environment, such as the Nazi state, without submitting to either one at the expense of the other. In Theresienstadt, Baeck "had given away nothing of himself," he remained "proud, fearless, dispassionate" (Friedlander, 1968, p. 217). For Bettelheim and Baeck, the most important dimension for integration to take place was having a set of strongly felt, flexibly and creatively applied, transcendent-pointing moral beliefs and values. Such an outlook acted as a defense against personality disintegration. It should be stressed that for a person to have a more-or-less consistent set of beliefs and values requires a degree of prior existing integration (i.e., in "normal" life, before 1933 when Hitler came to power), thus emphasizing the dialectical and mutually reinforcing relationship between them. The firmer one's beliefs and values are, the clearer one is about what one can and cannot give up to the state and still maintain one's integration. Moreover, according to Bettelheim, with such a firmly held set of more-or-less consistent guiding beliefs

and values in place, one has an increased ability to make autonomous decisions—the capacity to distinguish what could be given up to the environment without compromising the inner self, and more generally, the capacity to solve inner conflicts between his desires and what the environment demands. Such autonomy in turn helps the individual maintain, and strengthen his integration.

4) Remaining human is one of those phrases that can have a wide range of meanings depending on one's social and historical context (e.g., what "language game" one is lodged in).[4] By remaining human I mean it as Terrence Des Pres, a scholar of the Holocaust, uses the term in his extraordinary study of death camp inmates, where he equates staying human with keeping "life and decency . . . moral sense and dignity intact" (Des Pres, 1976, pp. 5, 16). The philosopher Tzvetan Todorov likens remaining human with the capacity "to care about others" (Todorov, 1996, p. 81). Bettelheim believed, as did Primo Levi, Jean Améry, Viktor E. Frankl, Elie Wiesel, and Anna Pawełczyńska (all Auschwitz survivors), H. G. Adler and Leo Baeck (Theresienstadt survivors) among others, that the central struggle for the inmate was the problem of "retaining one's humanity" (Bettelheim, 1960, p. 158).

5) Following Polish-American social psychologist, Milton Rokeach, by beliefs, I mean:

> Any simple proposition or unconscious, inferred from what a person says or does, capable of being preceded by the phrase 'I believe that . . .' The context of a belief may describe an object or situation as true or false; evaluate it as good or bad; or advocate a certain course of action as desirable or undesirable. Whether or not the content of a belief describe, evaluate or advocate action, or to do all three, all beliefs are predispositions to action.
>
> *(Rokeach, 1968, p. 450)*

Accordingly, says Rokeach, a belief system represents the total universe of a person's beliefs about the physical world, social world and the self. We can thus say that Baeck had a belief system, a traditional, Jewish one. However, Baeck was a liberal theologian so that some of his rationales reflected this outlook even though he lived as if he were a traditional Jew from what I can discern. For example, Baeck was a "liberal. He favor[ed] change in the 'law' [*halacha*] to allow 'commandment' to become more evident" (Borowitz, 1983, p. 70). This may in part, be because Baeck like Martin Buber cared more about a person living in sanctity than on achieving a unified, integrated intellectual worldview (Borowitz, 1983).[5]

6) A value is:

> A type of belief, centrally located within one's total belief system, about how one ought, or ought not, to behave, or about some end state of existence worth, or not worth, attaining. Values are thus abstract ideals, positive or negative, not tied to any specific attitude, object or situation, representing a person's beliefs about ideal modes of conduct and ideal terminal goals.
>
> *(Rokeach. p. 454)*

7) When the individual is faced with an extremely confusing, rapidly changing, contingent reality, when his routine and valued modes of thought and acting (i.e., his beliefs and values) are in the process of being destroyed, he feels himself to be in what Bruno Bettelheim calls an "extreme situation"—a social context in which the inmate is suddenly, massively and decisively threatened with the destruction of his world, fostering intense death anxiety. Indeed, Hájková describes everyday life in Theresienstadt and the atmosphere as one of "deprivation [e.g., of food], fear [e.g., of deportation], and terror" [e.g., of public hangings] (2020, p. 174).

I will be applying the aforementioned definitions throughout this book as well as liberally drawing from Bettelheim, the only full-length, psychoanalytically oriented study of life inside the concentration camp, and by extension, the concentration camp society of Nazi Germany (with its extreme, oppressive controls). While Theresienstadt was a ghetto it has some psychological overlap with other types of camps, especially in terms of the inmate existing in an extreme situation.

Baeck's Autonomy, Integration and Humanity in Nazi Germany

Above all else, Baeck viewed himself as a rabbi, that is, a spiritual leader, teacher and scholar. In fact, on his tombstone is inscribed in Hebrew, *Migesa Rabbonim*, "out of rabbinic ancestry." Baeck's narrative of self-identity had at its center his pastoral work. By pastoral work, I mean what is pertinent to the giving of spiritual guidance to his flock. Baeck appeared to view his pastoral work and scholarship as a "calling" as opposed to a "job" or "career." These are important distinctions that in part, broadly explain Baeck's overall motivational set, thus they deserve further comment.

As sociologists Bellah et al. (1986) first pointed out in their bestselling book, *Habits of the Heart: Individualism and Commitment in American Life*, a person with a "job" orientation to work is geared toward earning a living for himself and his family in order to prosper and to maximize the amount of their leisure time. In other words, work is viewed strictly as a practical means to a financial end. Moreover, his sense of self is mainly defined by financial success, security "and all that money can buy" (p. 66). A "career" is a way to advance oneself in terms of accomplishment, status and prestige. Such people mainly work in order to move up the hierarchical ladder, to be promoted, a competitive process they very much enjoy. The sense of self that is associated with a career is characterized by a broader kind of success than a job in that by attaining a degree of expanding power and competency, work itself becomes a way of sustaining self-esteem (Bellah et al., 1986). Individuals who have a "job" and "career" orientation toward work tend to have personal identities that do not significantly overlap with the actual work they do; to a large extent they view what they do at work as distinct from the rest of their life (Berg et al., 2010). They narrate their lives in terms of having a "work self" and a "non-work self," and rarely do they feel they are a "whole" or "complete self." While Baeck may have had a job and career motivational set earlier in his career as a community rabbi, at least to some extent, his outlook and behavior while in Nazi Germany strongly suggests that he viewed his pastoral and scholarly work as a calling.

A "calling" is a work orientation in which a person views their work as deeply satisfying and socially beneficial. That is, an individual chooses an occupation that he "feels drawn to pursue," often powerfully. He anticipates it to be "intrinsically enjoyable and meaningful," especially as a socially useful endeavor, and he views it "as a central part of his identity" (Berg et al., p. 973). As Bellah and colleagues noted, such work "constitutes a practical ideal of activity and character that makes a person's work morally inseparable from his or her life," and it links the person not only more intensely to his co-workers but to the larger community (Bellah et al., 1986). Indeed, as Friedlander noted, Baeck was "true to himself, to his calling as a teacher, a rabbi" (1968, p. 4). That is, for Baeck serving his flock was the source of character and fulfilment. He found his work to be a spiritual and ethical activity which was vital to his personality integration.

Mystery and Commandment

Baeck's "extraordinary character" (Meyer, 1999, p. 107) is lodged in the best of a traditional Jewish outlook, but with a few twists, such as the fact that he was associated with the liberal school of Jewish thought, while he lived as if he were a traditional Jew (as with Franz Rosenzweig he was something of an "orthoprax," that is, correct conduct, but having a non-traditional religious consciousness). Perhaps it is through his notions of "mystery and commandment" that we can get a glimpse of what made this man tick. For as Friedlander notes, mystery and commandment "must be understood as the basis of Baeck's personality. And conversely it tells us a great deal about Baeck" (1968, p.167). That is, Baeck "was a truly outstanding figure whose life and teaching blend together and can only be understood as one" (Friedlander, 1968, p. 49). The essay *Mystery and Commandment*, "was the description of the inner human experience, man's inner feelings as he encounters the commanding mystery of the holy, as he learns from that which is real that which is to be realized" (Friedlander, 1968, p. 170). As Baeck noted, mystery refers to "the knowledge of what is real," while commandment refers to "the knowledge of what is to be realized" (Baeck, 1981a [1958], p. 171). Baeck elaborates on the important difference between mystery and commandment:

> When man wants to be certain of his existence, when he therefore listens intently for the meaning of his life and life in general, and he thus feels the presence of something lasting, of some reality beneath the surface ['the arms of eternity'], then he experiences the mystery.
>
> And when man looks beyond the present day, when he wishes to give his life direction and lead it toward a goal, when he thus grasps that which defines his life and is clear about it, then he is always confronted with the commandment,

> the task, that which is to realize. The foundation of life is the mystery; the way of life is the revealed. The one is from God; the other to be achieved by man.
>
> *(Baeck, 1981a [1958], pp. 171–172)*

Most importantly, says Baeck, "the unity of both experiences in the human soul constitutes Jewish piety and Jewish wisdom; the meaning of life reveals itself here in this form" (1981a [1958], p. 174). In other words, "Both, mystery as well as commandment, represent certainty of life, the certainty of the self" (1981a [1958], p. 172).

Mystery and commandment can also be described as humility and reverence. Humility says Baeck, is his recognition that his life is framed by infinity and eternity, by that which transcends all human knowledge and apprehension, and surpasses all that is natural and existent. One's life is absolutely dependent on the unknowable, unnamable, unfathomable and unthinkable God. God, "is He in whom is all being, and God is also He that is positively different" (Baeck, 1981a [1958], p. 175). God is the "'I and Thou'" of man" (Baeck, 1948, p. 151). "God does not reveal Himself, but He reveals commandment and grace" (Meyer, 2021, p. 7).

Reverence in this context is man's feeling that something higher confronts him; and is ethically superior and therefore makes demands and directs, speaks to man and necessitates his reply, his autonomous decision. Such reverence is the recognition of the holy, "that which is infinitely and eternally commanding" (Baeck, 1981a [1958], p. 172). As Levinas explains, holiness (or saintliness), which was always his main interest, "this holiness . . . the supreme perfection . . . which cedes one place to the other" was what characterized "humanity" at its best (Levinas, 2001, p. 183). Baeck would quite likely agree with Levinas on this claim: "The pointed path to God is by way of our fellow-man." Moreover, the teachers of the Talmud "declared that this recognition of our fellow-man is the 'essence of the Torah'" (Baeck, 1958, p. 57).

Baeck associated the "essence of Judaism" with biblical prophecy, that is, the direct and immediate experience of God's presence (mystery) and the command to worship Him (commandment), a perspective he borrowed from the poet, philosopher and physician, Rabbi Judah Halevi (born *c.* 1075, died 1141). The Prophets were probably the world's first social critics, commanded by God to speak truth to power and to challenge morally corrupt leaders (Sacks, 2024a). Said Baeck, what made the prophets "unique",

> was the call which they experienced, the commandment that came to them to carry out the work of God, to form a new humanity and the future. It was the realization that they had been appointed to stand up for the one, the essential thing, against their nation and their time that constituted their unique quality and gave them their importance to the world.
>
> *(Baeck, 1958, p. 11)*

Thus, the essence of Judaism is a dialectic "polarity" (Baeck, 1981a [1958], p. 174), "a religion of polarity" (Friedlander, 1968, p. 141) between mystery and command. As Simon further notes, the commands, says Baeck, do not inevitably form a system of commandments like the time-honored *halacha* (Jewish law) which demands a required and fixed way of living; rather these commands appear occasionally "in the form of instructions for action like flashes of lightning that break through the cloud covering the divine mystery" (Simon, 2024, n.p.). A kind of spontaneous seeing of relations. Thus, according to Baeck, the religion of polarity must be comprehended with reference to the people Israel. Such a religion is one of experience, a humanistic theology which confirms God's existence clearly in ancient Jewish terms (Friedlander, 1968).

The upshot of the aforementioned in terms of how Baeck lived his life is put succinctly:

> Whoever experiences both [mystery and commandment], both in unity, lives in the world and yet is different, is different and yet is in the world, lives for other men and with other men and yet within himself, within himself and yet also for other men and hence also with them. This is the gift and possession of Judaism.
>
> *(Baeck, 1981a [1958], p. 184)*

Indeed, Baeck was described by those who knew him as a man who had an inner center of gravity that made him largely immune to the Nazi assault in terms of maintaining his integrity and self-respect, including directly after *Kristallnacht* (1938). Meyer (2021) noted, "And his personal morality was never in doubt. One might differ with him on this or that matter, but one did not doubt his integrity" (p. 50). As Baker describes it,

> Eva Reichmann [who lived in Berlin] remembered being in a group called before the Gestapo. Jews were not allowed to sit down in the Nazi officials' presence. Baeck advanced before them, as if to place his body between the Nazi and his fellow Jews. 'He stood there like a rock,' said Eva Reichmann. 'He was beyond death. Nothing could touch him.' That was probably the secret of his strength. Once Natalie [his beloved wife] had died [in 1937, Baeck was 63], no hurt could touch him.
>
> *(Baker 1978, p. 217).*[6]

To his friends and visitors from abroad, Baeck breathed "cheerfulness and faith, and maintained the same serenity of spirit" following the Nazis coming to power (Baker, 1978, p. 151). A fellow ghetto inmate noted that "Leo Baeck was untouched by Theresienstadt. He never was really there" (Baker, 1978, p. 287). In other words, Baeck resided in another dimension of the spirit while at the same time being politically astute, "he frequently showed tactical skill but was nevertheless unable to prevent evil" (Adler, 2022 [1955], p. 215).

Baker further reports that one of his friends who visited Baeck while living in London described him as "unchanged and unbroken" (Baker, 1978, p. 319), again suggesting that Baeck was situated in a different way of being-in-the-world compared to many other survivors of the Holocaust. In fact, as I have said, while incarcerated in Theresienstadt, Baeck was described as "proud, fearless, dispassionate," sometimes generating criticism because he personified these virtues (Friedlander, 1968, p. 217).

Thus, before his deportation from Germany, while in Theresienstadt, and after his liberation and living in London, Baeck appears to have remained more-or-less the same, at least in terms of the main thrust of his existential grounding. As Bettelheim noted about his concentration camp experiences in Dachau and Buchenwald in 1938,

> If I should try sum up in one sentence what my main problem was during the whole time I spent in the camps, it would be: to protect my inner self in such a way that if, by any good fortune, I should regain my liberty, I would be approximately the same person I was when deprived of liberty.
>
> *(Bettelheim, 1960, p. 126)*

By this standard Baeck appeared to be successful at maintaining his "core" beliefs and values, beliefs and values that in part, constituted his sense of self.

Baeck did not feel humiliated while living in the concentration camp society (i.e., Nazi Germany with its cruel domination) (Marcus, 1999). Indeed, as Friedlander (1968) notes "Germany was in fact, a concentration camp" (p. 38). As the above eyewitnesses noted, in a sense, Baeck wasn't there, rather he lived in a world in which his religious beliefs and values nurtured and stabilized him. This was often not the case with other German Jews who felt humiliated by their ordeal of suffering.[7] By humiliation I mean, following Rorty (1989), that when the story that a person has been telling himself about his life, when the narrative which constitute his self-identity has been rendered almost completely meaningless, it cuts deeply into his motivation to carry on. As Meyer (2021) noted for example, after Kristallnacht, the November 1938 pogrom, "reported suicides accounted for more than half of Jewish burials" (p. 128).[8] Baeck too, was probably traumatized by Kristallnacht, saying "How often have the scenes of that night returned to us, whether we wished it or not, that night . . . when the great blasphemy took place—the destruction of the synagogues" (Baker, 1978, p. 229).

As I will detail later, according to Bettelheim (and survivors of Auschwitz, such as Levi, Améry and Wiesel, and others.) it was the non-political, non-religious, middle-class prisoners who had the greatest difficulty responding to the initial period of internment, and the period up to deportation to Theresienstadt (and then to Auschwitz), because they had lost the foundations of their self-respect. Their self-esteem had heavily relied on a status and respect that came with their positions, depended on their jobs, on being head of a family, or similar external factors. Without external structures to prop them up they collapsed into despair soon after their arrival into the camps and to some extent, prior to deportation (Bettelheim, 1960, pp. 120–122).

> It can become completely shattering to a person's integration when the system of beliefs on which he relied for integration . . . not only lets him down, but worse, is about to destroy him psychologically and physically. Then nothing seems left that can offer protection. Furthermore, we now no longer can feel confident that we will be able to ever again to know reliably what to trust, and what to defend against.
>
> *(Bettelheim, 1979, p. 10)*

In other words, these inmates, without their familiar world of meaning—their social position, prestige and power to command—without a sense of their world as orderly, stable, continuous and comprehensible, were unable to maintain their prior narrative of self-identity. Their security of their being was threatened, and their sense of self was shattered (Weinstein, 1980). Moreover, as Erich Fromm has pointed out, without the props on which their self-esteem and sense of identity rested, these non-political, non-religious middle-class inmates collapsed "morally like a deflatable balloon" (Fromm, 1973, p. 86). In a word, these inmates felt humiliated. In contrast as I said earlier, Baeck had deeply internalized, strongly felt, flexibly and creatively applied, transcendent-pointing moral beliefs and values, allowing him to sustain his autonomy, integration and humanity, at least relatively speaking. Creativity is very important in all of this, for as psychoanalyst Donald Winnicott noted, "it is creative apperception more than anything else that makes the individual feel that life is worth living" (1971, p. 71). Baeck had a similar view, when he emphasized that life is not only a question of new experiences, but also of actualizations, of creativity (Friedlander, 1968). The aim of Baeck's ethical thought, like all ethical thought, was to assist him in constructing a world of meaning that will be his world, one in which he has a social, cultural and personal life (Williams, 1993). Put differently, to be largely "unconcerned with what others may do to you, even when your life is at stake, because you are committed to the truth of your own life, is the supreme act of personal autonomy" (Berkovits, 1979, p. 74).

Baeck's religion of polarity was in part based on three paradoxes as outlined in *The Essence of Judaism* (1948). As Friedlander summarizes the matter, these paradoxes are at the center of the Baeckian "system": (1) Man's awareness of his finitude and his infinite strivings and hopes; (2) His mindfulness of his complete dependency upon God and his independence of ethical action; (3) These two paradoxes merge together in the paradox of a life of incalculable worth which is however, found wanting before God's judgement (Friedlander, 1968). The religious person ideally lives with these paradoxes in a creative tension; indeed, says Baeck, there is "a constant struggle between proximity and distance, between becoming and being, between temporal beginning and eternal end" (Baeck, 1966 [1947]), p. 138).

Other polarities mentioned by Baeck that compose his "twofoldedness that is found in all aspects of the world and man,"[9] include, for example, mystery and ethics, man and humanity, optimism and pessimism, the transient and the eternal, the rational and nonrational, nearness and distance, and the particular and the universal (Friedlander, 1968, pp. 184, 185, 224).

Living mindfully of the aforementioned three paradoxes centrally involves one's commitment to ethical monotheism, a notion that Baeck appropriated from the neo-Kantian philosopher Hermann Cohen. As Borowitz (1983) noted, "Baeck found ethical monotheism to be the essence of Judaism" (p. 56). However, Baeck diverged from Cohen in lodging his explication of Judaism not only on the sense of the ethical but also on religious consciousness that teaches about God. Religion, for Baeck was more than the scientific-ethical rationalism as the neo-Kantians' believed (religion as reason), but was a unique human experience that could best be accessed through careful phenomenological description of inner experience (Borowitz, 1983, pp. 56, 57). Said Baeck, "To seek God is to strive for good; to find God is to do good" (Friedlander, 1968, p. 68). One of Baeck's rabbinic colleagues, Bruno Italiener, described Baeck as "a man who drew his full strength out of his living belief in God, out of his impassioned love for the Jewish people" (Friedlander, 1968, p.39). That is, for Baeck, Judaism was a communal way of being, a way of life lived in the presence of God (Berkovits, 1979).

Indeed, Baeck was committed to the ethical outlook and behavior, years before Levinas made the claim that "responsibility [i.e., ethics] is the essential, primary and fundamental structure of subjectivity" [ethics as first philosophy[. (Levinas, 1985, p. 95). Levinas did not use the word "ethics" until the 1950s (Katz, 2014). Baeck's conduct during the Nazi years, including while incarcerated in Theresienstadt, was characterized as ethical in the extreme. For example, before he was incarcerated, while living under Nazi rule he felt it was his moral obligation to "save the young" through emigration, "and succor the old" through strengthening their cultural and spiritual life of those who remained in Nazi Germany (Baker, 1978, p. 152). This involved "negotiating" with his Nazi overlords in a gradually shrinking moral field of vision and action. However, said Baeck, "Fate comes and fate goes, but justice remains" (Baker, 1978). As Feller noted, as Baeck was the leader of the German Jewish community, he thus "had to form policy and coordinate actions in a constantly shrinking sphere of action" (Feller, 2024, p. 73).

An example of Baeck's impressive character was described many years later by a young rabbi, Joachim Prinz, who lived in Berlin in 1930:

> Why select Leo Baeck to head the national Jewish organization? The Gestapo officials could not talk to Leo Baeck the way they talked to me. He represented the dignity, the history of the Jewish people. He represented that which in Jewish existence is eternal. He commanded respect, even from the Gestapo.
>
> *(Baker, 1978, p. 162)*

Feller cites the same Eva Reichman mentioned earlier who reported the story that,

> Baeck told a Gestapo officer that he was not afraid to walk the streets of Berlin with the yellow badge. Some strangers, Baeck said, would make risky small gestures, smuggling a cigarette, a chocolate, or an apple to his pocket or quickly shaking his hand.
>
> *(Feller, 2024, p. 109)*

Feller emphasizes Baeck's alleged behavior which shows defiance and agency, the latter which is a sub-species of autonomy in my view.

In another instance, Baeck scorned the Nazis openly. According to Pasachoff (1992), the Gestapo demanded that Baeck come to their headquarters on the Sabbath, but Baeck refused to go. He said, "I'm not in the habit of showing up to an office on Saturday. On the Sabbath I go to services" (p. 152).

Baeck performed other gestures which were quiet acts of defiance and autonomy while living in the concentration camp society. For example, before 1933 he had a daily routine in which he awakened at about five o'clock each morning and prayed. Then, he would study a page of the Talmud, then read one act from a Greek play in the original Greek, and only then, would he be ready to start his day proper (Friedlander, 1968). However, during "the Nazi years, when his responsibilities did not allow sufficient time for his studies, he changed his waking hour from five o'clock to four, so he would still have time for hours of study" (Baker, 1978, pp. 26–27). Prayer and learning were ways of transporting himself to a different dimension of the spirit, an island of freedom and transcendence which sustained a sense of biographical continuity.

From 1933 to 1938 Baeck also set aside time for translating (three times) the Gospels from Greek into Hebrew, in order "to sift the oldest parts by Hebrew-speaking Jews, including Jesus himself, from later extensions and accretions" (Baker, 1978, p. 202). Baeck's creed, says Baker was "that one continually invest something more of himself each day" (Baker, 1978). Such an outlook helped him to psychologically survive.

Baeck fought antisemitism by demonstrating and strengthening the Jewish elements in Christianity (Feller, 2024). Baeck also began writing his most complex book, *This People Israel: The Meaning of Jewish Existence*, under the threat of Nazism and the stress of Theresienstadt (Feller, 2024). In other words, during the Nazi period, Baeck attempted to maintain a semblance of his former life, his way of being-in-the-world, and by doing so reinforced his ontological security (e.g., his self-esteem, self-continuity and self-coherence) amidst Nazi assault. Following existential psychiatrist/psychoanalyst, R.D. Laing, by ontological security, I mean a person's sense of presence in the world as real, alive, whole, and in a temporal sense, continuous. Says Laing, such a basically ontological secure person will encounter all the dangers of life, social, ethical, spiritual, biological from a centrally secure sense of his own and other peoples' reality and identity (Laing,

1962). Such a person has a trust in his own self-efficacy and ability to influence the world he lives in. As the social psychologist Albert Bandura who originated the concept noted, self-efficacy references an individual's heartfelt belief in his/her capacity to perform behaviors needed to produce specific performance accomplishments.

Baeck viewed spiritual death in terms of it being "a loss of the ability to overcome fate and to create one's life ever anew" (Meyer, 2021, p. 64). In Baeck's view, "the ability to renew one's life was the true religiosity" (Meyer, 2021, p. 65). And this religiosity was demonstrated by a mindfulness of moral obligation. Baeck often quoted from Ralph Waldo Emerson: "Let your faith be seen in your deeds" (Meyer, 2021, p. 71).

Another example of Baeck standing up for himself against the Nazi authorities occurred while living in Berlin when he was arrested and briefly imprisoned (probably in a holding cell) five times:

> Baeck exploited his international reputation in subsequent dealings with the Gestapo; in the five times he was arrested he refused to eat non-kosher food, forcing his captors either to find him food that did not violate the tradition or to buy kosher food, rather than allow him to starve.
>
> *(Baker, 1978, p. 208)*

Feller (2024) suggests that when Baeck was forced by the Nazis to write what a 1200-page "contested manuscript" (he had two competent co-writers), awkwardly titled *Development of the Legal Position of Jews in Europe, Primarily in Germany from Antiquity to the Beginning of the Age of Enlightenment* (henceforth Legal Position) (pp. 111–112), he was in fact engaged in a form of intellectual resistance. While I have not read the German manuscript, I tend to agree with Feller's analysis of it based on my understanding of Baeck, the man:

> My argument that the Legal Position was not written *for* the resistance does not mean it is not a work *of* resistance. Treating it as intellectual forced labor highlights the conditions under which it was written and allows a move beyond the dichotomy of resistance or collaboration. Moments of subversion in the manuscript are rare, and at most take the form of omissions or refusal to engage, rather than outright counterhistory. That is explained through the precarious position of the authors.
>
> *(Feller, 2024, p. 117)*

Feller provides an analysis of the manuscript which is most interesting as Baeck covers a number of pertinent discussions of, for example, antisemitism and Zionism. For our purpose, however, what is most significant is that Baeck found an intellectual way to elevate Judaism and the Jewish people without inviting Nazi reprisal, a demonstration of defiance of the Nazi regime.

Baeck was also arrested in 1937 when the Gestapo ordered the closure of the B'nai B'rith, a fraternal Jewish cultural association, and removed its property, valued in the millions. At the time Baeck still was the national president of the association, and the Gestapo placed before him a statement in which he consented to relinquish all the B'nai B'rith's property to the Nazi government. "I refuse to sign," Baeck recollected. "Thus, their act stood as the theft which it was" (Baker, 1978, p. 208).

In another instance, Baeck pragmatically and silently protested the Nazi assault. The German authorities ordered that the Jews should relinquish all of their silver, this included ceremonial pieces. As Baker further notes, in Baeck's residence there were a few religious objects, many of which belonged to his late wife Natalie and her family. "Rather than let the Nazis find them and melt them down, Baeck rented a row boat, went out into the harbor where the Elbe River met the channel, and dumped them." Apparently, he chose that spot because it had tides, and he could feel sure the silver mementos would never be retrieved again (Baker, 1978, p. 240). Said Baeck, "The Nazis could take our property but not our spirit" and sense of community (Baker, 1978, p. 194).

In yet another example of the many assaults on Jewish dignity, the authorities attempted to subvert Jewish leadership by forcing them to act against their religious convictions. For example, shortly after the outbreak of war in 1939, it was ordered that all Jews must personally return their radios to the police station on the Day of Atonement (Yom Kippur, the holiest day of the year for the Jewish people), failure to comply with the order was severely punishable. "Nonetheless, Baeck did not comply. Only after the conclusion of the Day of Atonement did Baeck return his radio" (Meyer, 2021, p. 136). Meyer further notes, as Baeck arrived, "he heard one police officer say to his colleague, 'Didn't I tell you that Rabbi Baeck wouldn't turn up on his holy day?'" Apparently, the police did not report Baeck's act of defiance to the Gestapo, and Baeck never received any punishment (Meyer, 2021).

Baeck also composed some prayers that were to be read in all of the synagogues on Shabbat Nachamu and Yom Kippur. Shabbat Nachamu: ("Sabbath of Consolation") is the Sabbath[10] following the fast of Tisha B'Av,[11] so called because of the passage "Nachamu" (Isaiah, 40:1) read for the Haftorah (from the Prophets). In August 1935, before the Nuremberg Laws were operational, he wrote the following for Shabbat Nachamu. I am quoting the short prayer in full to give the reader a "feel" for what Baeck was aiming for. Wrote Baeck, "Comfort, oh comfort, My People",

> That is what today's Sabbath calls to us. From when in these days when we are forced to traverse a flood of insults shall comfort arise? It arises from the answer that our faith, that our honor, that our youth give us.
>
> Against all insults we set the majestic dignity of our religion, [against] all offences our steady persistence in pursuing the paths of our Judaism, in following its commandments.

> True Honor is what each person grants to himself; he gives it to himself through a life that is unimpeachable and pure, modest and honest, as well as through a life of that self-control which is the mark of inner strength. Our honor is before God; it alone will endure.
>
> Our youth—does not it not give us a model of unpretentiousness and courage, of mastering this difficult life in new ways? Let us, parents and teachers, raise up a generation strong and hard against itself, ready to be of assistance to everyone else, with a strong body and a fresh spirit, faithful and firm, rooted in Judaism.
>
> Let yourselves not be cast down and let yourselves not be embittered. Trust in the One to whom the ages belong.
>
> *(Meyer, 2021, p. 105).*

As Meyer notes in his analysis of the prayer, Baeck is suggesting three aspects where the Jews who heard or read the prayer could affirm themselves: (1) The Nazis could not take away their faith in God and doing his commandments; (2) the honor that was self-generated as opposed to the dishonor that was imposed on them from the outside; (3) a Jewish youth that would be strengthened by its ordeal of suffering, and was dedicated to the best interests of the larger community (Meyer, 2021).

The main purpose of this prayer was to comfort and inspire the Jews who heard it amidst a state that had begun to tighten its diabolical hold on the Jewish community, leading to an upsurge of anxiety and depression. The fact that this prayer was read on Shabbat Nachamu made its meaning much more poignant and powerful.

A few weeks later, after the Nuremberg Laws came into operation, Baeck composed a second prayer that was to be read on the Day of Atonement (Yom Kippur), October 6, 1935. Yom Kippur, the holiest day in the Jewish calendar, emphasizes atonement and repentance for sins against God. One part of the prayer reads as follows:

> In this hour, all Israel stand before its God, who is judging and forgiving. Before Him, we shall all examine our ways, examine, what we have done and what we have neglected, examine where we have gone and where we have remained distant. Wherever we have failed, we wish to confess openly; 'we have sinned,' and we shall pray with steadfast resolve to repent before God: forgive us!
>
> We stand before our God. With the same strength . . . with which we have acknowledged our sins, the sins of the individual and those of the community we speak with feeling of abhorrence that we see deep beneath our feet the lie directed against us and the slander of our faith and its witnesses.
>
> *(Feller, 2024, p. 95)*

As Meyer (2021) notes, in this prayer Baeck emphasizes that Jews are not to be held accountable to the state in the face of the brutal Nazism, they are only accountable to God, the only one who can legitimately judge their behavior during the year. Baeck wrote, "To Him we bow down, and we stand upright before humans," in other words Baeck was saying that only the Jew can define who he is, not the Nazi authorities (Meyer, 2021, p. 107). This prayer was probably not read in many places because of the political situation, including Baeck's periods in jail after arrest by the Gestapo.

What is important in part to understand about these two prayers is that they represent Baeck's religious outlook on his awful situation as a Jew living in Nazi Germany. Most importantly what Baeck was asserting, as a form of defiance and protest, was that no Jew should align himself with anyone else's definition/description of his person, in particular the dehumanizing definition that was imposed by the Nazis. Baeck was also advocating drawing from Jewish spirituality to fend off the lies that the Nazis were saying about Jews. His prayers were a form of reasoned, though passionately felt, self-affirmation amidst the slanderous allegations of the Nazis. As Feller (2024) noted about the Yom Kippur prayer, "Baeck transformed the moment of standing before God in repentance to a moment of protest and self-assertion in the name of God" (p. 96).

As the head of German Jewry in the Nazi period (before deportation to Theresienstadt), Baeck had to make a number of difficult moral decisions, decisions that were, and still are in some quarters, controversial. For example, he was criticized for not evacuating more Jews from Nazi Germany while it was still feasible (*New World Encyclopedia*, 2022). It would appear that Baeck initially focused on "spiritual resistance," that is, the strengthening of cultural and religious life for those who did not emigrate. He also was "negotiating" with the Nazis, such that he and the others "played for time" so that lives could be saved. Baeck understood that emigration of young people was essential and was the best guarantee for the future of the Jewish people. As I said earlier, according to one of his biographers, Leonard Baker, Beck's two-pronged approach was to "save the young" through emigration "and succor the old" through strengthening the cultural and spiritual life of those who remained in Nazi Germany. Considering the terrible context of Baeck's decision, his chosen course of action appeared to have been realistic and reasonable, intended to assist the majority of the Jewish community.

More seriously, while living in Berlin, he had kept to himself the grim knowledge that Jews in the East were being murdered by *Einsatzgruppen* and others [mobile killing units of the SS and SD], administering death by asphyxiation and by mass shootings. There is also the allegation that Baeck erred by not disclosing that the "resettlement trains" were in fact going to death camps (this was occurring during incarceration in Theresienstadt, a transit camp to Auschwitz). In Baeck's view he decided on this course of action in part because he did not want to dash the inmate's hope and also to curtail possible suicidal attempts. Said Baeck, "To destroy all hope would lead to despair and death in Theresienstadt" (Friedlander, 1995, p. xii). Having learned by about August 1943 of the horrible fate that awaited those packed into the cattle cars exiting Theresienstadt, the question for Baeck was, should he make that knowledge public (Meyer, 2021). After the war Baeck explained:

> I did not know whether [the transports were going] to Auschwitz. But that the intention was probably to murder immediately whoever was not fit for hard labor and to let those who were capable of working for the war machine eventually perish from hunger and deprivation—that I knew was the Gestapo's goal. At the time, I was caught up in the pangs of conscience: Should one shorten the agonies of those destined for departing transports through self-initiated massacre or give some, even if only very few, a chance for survival? I finally said to myself: Even if only a single person will survive, we may not sacrifice that person.
>
> *(Meyer, 2021, p. 163)*

Baeck further commented,

> I finally decided that no one should know. If the Council of Elders were informed, the whole camp would know within a few hours. Knowledge of death by gassing would only be harder, and death was not certain at all. There was the selection for slave labor and perhaps not all transports went to Auschwitz. So I decided not to tell anyone.
>
> *(Grobman, 1983, p. 252)*

As Meyer (2021) noted, when the war was over, Baeck found out that some of those deported from Theresienstadt had survived the death camps, his conscience was at least partly moderated, and he became convinced that he had made the correct decision. That is, says Meyer, a mass suicide brought about by despair would not have been a preferred outcome.

The great Protestant religious existentialist Paul Tillich, who knew, admired and respected Baeck, disagreed with Baeck:

> No one can fully judge the events within the concentration camp. But in a way, I would criticize Baeck for not giving the last iota of information which he possessed. If he did know that Auschwitz meant certain death, he should have spoken out. The full existential truth should always be made available, just as the incurable patient should always be told the full truth.
>
> *(Friedlander, 1968, p. 47)*[12]

There is no simple right or wrong answer regarding Baeck' decision, Tillich makes a convincing point but so does Baeck who always had the best interests of the inmates of Theresienstadt as his first priority. Perhaps, the Talmudic dictum applies here, "do not judge your fellow man until you have been put in his position" (Marcus, 2024, p. 24).

Hannah Arendt also criticized, if not attacked, Baeck's leadership of German Jewry during the Nazi period, infamously writing in *Eichman in Jerusalem: A Report on the Banality of Evil*, "in the eyes of both Jews and Gentiles [Baeck] was the 'Jewish Fuhrer.'" After being "reprimanded" by the illustrious historian/philosopher Gershom Scholem, Arendt felt regretful that she had used the provocative and obnoxious description of a man who personified human decency and removed the ill-conceived term from subsequent editions of her book (Meyer, 2021).

Baeck was also criticized because he used Jewish orderlies or helpers (including some young rabbinic students) to "round up" Jews for deportation in Berlin rather than the Nazis, he thought the latter would be much more brutal in the process. Some have claimed that Baeck and his entourage "cooperated" with the Nazis by engaging in these round-ups, but as not doing so would have made matters even worse for the Jews, such a criticism seems unfair. Baeck may have "cooperated" with the Nazis but he never "collaborated" with them, that is, he never sympathized with their ideology and behavior (Meyer, 2024). Raul Hilberg for example, in his masterpiece *The Destruction of the European Jews*, argues that because the Jewish leadership was controlled by the Nazis, the Jewish communal organization evolved into a self-destructive machine. Hannah Arendt picked up on this allegation claiming that there was widespread cooperation of the Jewish councils in the actual procedures of deportation to the death camps (Baker, 1978).[13] While it was the Jewish council that prepared the list of inmates to be deported. There is no evidence that Baeck participated in this decision-making.

The matter is hardly straightforward. While one can argue for both sides of the tough moral decisions that Baeck made, what is important from our point of view is the likely way Baeck engaged the decision-making process. It should be emphasized that living under the Nazis was not only a situation to be suffered; as in intense neurotic conflict, it also threatened Baeck's ability to make reasonable moral judgments. The Nazi assault challenged Baeck's "resources to provide a workable set of ethical criteria, normative guides to govern" his actions in the face of radical evil (Geertz, 1973, p. 106). Also, it is quite conceivable that the making of these impossible decisions must have been a form of suffering for Baeck.

As Baeck noted, "the wisdom of Judaism is that it sees life as a task imposed upon man by God. Suffering is part of that task; every creative individual experiences it" (Feller, 2024, p. 146). And as Friedlander pointed out, for Baeck "in the concentration camp [and in the concentration camp society], suffering became an ethical imperative in which God was present" (1968, p. 82). Thus, for Baeck, under Nazi rule, and for that matter in Theresienstadt, there was no "God is dead" approach put forth. As Baeck succinctly put it in *The Essence of Judaism*:

> Even when sufferings press hard upon man, he is to tread the path on which he himself decides. He is not merely to be locked in the straits of his affliction. Here he can show the great 'and yet' of his will to fulfill the commandment and

render proof of his reverence and his creative freedom; here he can rise to the heights of true human significance.

(Baeck, 1948, p. 138).[14]

Said Baeck, "We must affirm suffering with secure certainty; by turning it into an ethical imperative" (Friedlander, 1968, p. 82). That is, to the extent that one can transform one's suffering into other-directed, other-regarding and other-serving behavior then one has transcended the self, at least to some extent.

Baeck was deported to Theresienstadt on January 27, 1943. As Meyer (2021) recounts the event, the Nazis came for him early in the morning. Baeck recollected: "I was fully dressed when the bell rang at a quarter to six. Only the Gestapo would come at that hour. My housekeeper let in two men in civilian clothes.[15] One of them addressed me: 'We have orders to take you to Theresienstadt.'" Meyer notes that Baeck did not resist arrest, expecting that the day would come when he was to be deported. Meyer continues,

> But once again, he refused to be simply an object, passively drawn into their hands. He insisted on permission to write to relatives and friends and even made a request that some critics later displayed an obsessive clinging to bourgeois norms but was a way of raising himself morally above his captors: he would not go until he paid his gas and electric bills.
>
> *(Meyer, 2001, p. 144)*

I believe that Baeck paid his gas and electric bill for another reason, a noble one, as Friedlander suggests. Says Friedlander,

> That act can be seen as an expression of German pedantry or a Jewish sense of duty. Or it might be reminiscent of that famous scene in Plato's *Apology* where Socrates, putting the cup of hemlock to his lips, instructs his friends to pay his outstanding debts. In Baeck's case, everything we know about him suggests that the latter interpretation is more correct.
>
> *(Friedlander, 1995, p. xi)*

Baeck mentions two qualities of mind and heart that were critical to survival in Theresienstadt, but also to a lesser extent in Germany before his incarceraton. I am referring to the role of "ethical imagination" and "historical patience" (Baeck, 1947, p. 506). Ethical imagination,

> shapes the picture of the 'thou shalt,' the one picture of the inseparable ethical and social task, the picture of that humanity in which can alone be the goal, and the picture of the way leading to this goal. It is the imagination filled with great vision.
>
> *(Baeck, 1947)*

By historical patience Baeck means a,

> patience that is ready to begin from the beginning all over again; this is active patience. . . . But historical patience, which also endures and begins all over again, is something else something more. It thinks always of the ultimate and therefore in terms of centuries; its word is the word coined by Jewish genius: 'from generation to generation.' It is the patience of the endless way.
>
> *(Baeck, 1947)*

Baeck made the important point that imagination and patience were crucial to remaining human in Theresienstadt but also, I believe, while living in concentration camp society. Baeck further defined imagination as "the vision that ever again and in spite of everything makes him see a future." He defined patience as "this power of resilience that did not let the will to live give way" (Baker, 1978, p. 295). Baeck, always the optimist, believed in his reading of Jewish history, including the present diabolical circumstances of living in Nazi Germany. That is, he believed in his desire, and the desire of all self-affirming Jews, to fulfill God's commandments to live as unwavering. In this way, he, and Jews in general, maintained his imagination and patience (Baker, 1978).

I have indicated that Baeck was an all-pervasive optimist. Indeed, this is one of the qualities of mind and heart that helped him survive his ordeal of suffering more-or-less intact as a person. Judaism for Baeck was a "religion of optimism, the closed optimism of ethics which is not founded in the finite man but in the one God whose essence is the moral law" (Friedlander, 1968, p. 79). As Baeck noted,

> The Messianic idea also completes the conception of reverence toward man: it culminates in the idea of reverence toward humanity. The grand style here enters into history. This is the source of the optimism of Israel's religion. . . . It is the optimism that is contained in decision for God, the optimism that becomes the commandment and therefore sometimes demands heroism and martyrdom.
>
> *(Baeck, 1958, p. 69)*

However, while Baeck has been characterized as an optimist, his general outlook may be more exactingly described as hopeful. That is, there is a difference between optimism and hopefulness, as the great theoretician of the psychology of hope, neo-Socratic philosopher Gabriel Marcel has noted (Marcel was a believing convert to Catholicism). I therefore want to discuss the likely character of Baeck's hope structure. This will require grasping Marcel's phenomenology of hoping, which, while difficult to comprehend for most people, is surely worth it. This is especially the case, for as Pruyser (1963) notes, hope is a "boundary concept," and therefore it straddles several disciplines (e.g., philosophy, positive psychology, theology).

Baeck as an Example of Marcelian Hoping

As Baeck noted after his incarceration, after he was "imprisoned and held in the clutch of despair. To me, America has always meant hope. We could live without food and without clothes, but we could not live without hope, and so long as there was an America, we knew that it would be our salvation" (Meyer, 2021, p. 185). Moreover, said Baeck,

> Perhaps, you don't appreciate an intangible such as faith until you have lived, almost without hope, in a concentration camp. But I can testify that the hours which my doomed congregation in the concentration camp Theresienstadt spent in prayer and study were hours of contentment, the hours of freedom.
>
> *(Feller, 2024, p. 134)*[16]

Said Baeck in *This People Israel*:

> When the strength within man becomes aware of itself, when it draws in new breath, it becomes hope and it gives man the certainty of that which will endure. Hope is a reconciliation of the finite with that which remains.
>
> *(Baeck, 1964, p. 161)*

And finally, in his discussion of Moses Hess, (d. 1875), the German-Jewish philosopher and champion of Labor Zionism, Baeck reflects on hope:

> He taught the Jews to see in themselves not hopes but *the* Hope, the one great hope, the moral, social hope, the hope in the unity of man, of all men by virtue of the right that God gives them. His time has come, and yet not come, for much depends on what future years can produce in the Jewish people.
>
> *(Baeck, 1957, p. 43)*

Hope, says Marcel,

> consists in asserting that there is at the heart of being, beyond all data, beyond all inventories and all calculations, a mysterious principle which is in connivance with me, which cannot but will that which I will, if what I will deserves to be willed and is, in fact, willed by the whole of my being.
>
> *(Marcel, 1995, p. 28)*[17]

Hope is thus an expression of that irrepressible human urge towards "something more," "something higher," "something better," towards transcendence. Transcendence refers to the "unknown and higher dimension of reality attainable through human experience" (Cain, 1979, p. 115), it "is engaged in the weaving of experience now in process, or, in other words, is an adventure now going forward" (Marcel, 1965, p. 52). Hope says Marcel is an "exigency," a fundamental impulse or striving of being, "a deep-rooted interior urge . . . an appeal," (Marcel, 2001 [1951], p. 37) and thus is one of the fundamental ways in which freedom is affirmed. Hope, when it is joined with a robust imagination (including in the Baeckian sense), generates the freedom to expand possibility (Lynch, 1965, p. 81). "I act freely if the motives of my act are in line with what I can legitimately regard as the structural features of my personality" (Marcel, 1973, p. 86). What needs to be emphasized here is that for Marcel hope is better conceived as "hoping," that is, the phenomenology of hope reveals that it is not simply a fixed idea that one possesses in one's head as it were, but rather it is a processive, emergent and renewable psychological and behavioral activity that tends to upsurge in particular challenging contexts,[18] in extreme situations of imprisonment, like in Theresienstadt. "Hope," says Marcel, "is a response to tragedy" (Pruyser, 1963, p. 86). Indeed, Baeck's view of his distressing, if not diabolical, situation while living in Nazi Germany, and especially while in Theresienstadt, personifies an outlook that is permeated with hoping, hoping for deliverance or salvation from Nazi brutality. That is, as Pruyser (1963) notes, in order to be able to hope one must first have a feeling of captivity by the human condition. The less life is felt as captivity, the less is a person vulnerable to hoping.

Marcel goes out of his way to distinguish hoping from desire. Desire is when one wishes or looks for a specific thing or entity. "Desire is centered on the 'self,' whereas hope is inseparable from love," from the inter-subjective (1973, p. 43). Indeed, Baeck's way of giving succor to those Jews who remained in Nazi Germany and in Theresienstadt (including non-Jews), affirm this distinction between hoping and desire. Optimism, that tendency to believe, expect, or hope that things will turn out well, is one of its most common expressions. Moreover, says Marcel,

> the optimist . . . always relies upon an experience which is not drawn from the most intimate and living part of himself, but, on the contrary is considered from a sufficient distance to allow certain contradictions to become alternate or fused in a general harmony.
>
> *(Marcel, 1965, p. 34)*[19]

The optimist then, relates to externals, outside the intimacy of the self. The optimist reasons: "If you could only see things as clearly as I do . . ." or, "If you could only adopt my viewpoint . . ." As Pruyser further notes, the hoping person, in contradistinction

> to the optimist [and the pessimist] remains part of the scheme of things. He is not distant from reality and from others; he appears to himself as being implied in a wider reality which transcends him. His attitude is one of modesty and humility before the nature of reality. Marcel says there is an aspect of chastity in hope.
>
> *(Pruyser, 1963, p. 89)*

The danger of such wishful thinking as in optimism is that it can be self-delusional, and Baeck did not engage in the delusional remolding of reality. He was more of a pragmatic realist. By contrast, hope is an "open-ended expectation in which one anticipates without knowing exactly what it is he is waiting or hoping for" (*New World Encyclopedia* 2022).[20]

In Baeck's case it was deliverance in some form from the Nazi ordeal of suffering. This distinction is the difference between "I hope that" and "I hope" says Marcel, between approaching my ordeal of suffering as a "problem," "something which I meet, which I find complete before me, but which I can heretofore lay siege to and reduce," as for example, in all scientific inquiry, versus a "mystery," "something in which I am myself involved, and it can therefore only be thought of as a sphere where the distinction between what is in me and what is before me loses its meaning and its initial validity," as in a life-threatening disease or imprisonment in a concentration camp or ghetto (1975, p. 117). Baeck believed in mystery, in the mysterious God, the unknowable, unnamable, unfathomable and unthinkable Almighty. Moreover, as Feller (2024) noted "the mystery in Judaism was posited against self-centeredness, the accompanying feeling of passivity, and the detachment from the world. Instead, it led to acting ethically" (p. 72).

One of the most important though counter-intuitive aspects of hoping is that in a certain sense, although it is co-fashioned by the hard "captivity" that is inevitably self-referential, it is an activity that moves against one's inordinate, infantile narcissism. As Marcel says, "speaking metaphysically, the only genuine hope is hope in what does not depend on ourselves, hope springing from humility and not from pride" (1995, p. 32). "Hope only escapes from a particular metaphysical ruling on condition that it transcends desire . . . that it does not remain centered upon the subject himself" (p. 66). "The more hope tends to reduce itself to a matter of dwelling on, or of becoming hypnotized over, something one has represented to oneself, the more the objection we have just formulated will be irrefutable" (p. 45). What I believe Marcel is in part getting at is that hoping is experienced by the hoper not as something he can determine or fashion on his own. While hoping does involve willing it is not simply an expression of this psychic process, for it lacks the feeling of ego enhancement of willing, the sense that it is a center of action and emotion (Pruyser, 1963, p. 88). Hoping requires a modicum of yielding to the insurmountable force "of nature outside of us, to the non-ego" (p. 92). As Marcel construes it, hoping is experienced as a kind of "gift," one that is felt as ultimately emanating from outside oneself; in religious terms, personified by Marcel's outlook, such a moment is called "grace," that gratuitous, infinite love, mercy, favor and goodwill shown to humankind by God.

Baeck had the capacity to endure his ordeal of suffering without falling into incapacitating fear and utter despair, as a mysterious upsurge of qualities of mind and heart that required great courage. "Courage, in the final analysis," says German neurologist/psychiatrist Kurt Goldstein somewhere, "is nothing but an affirmative answer to the shocks of existence, which must be borne for the actual realization of one's own inner nature." That Baeck was able to view his ordeal in this way and respond accordingly, at least to some degree and most of the time, were "found" qualities of character that were "co-produced," perhaps by God's perceived presence.

Hope, then, unlike despair and depression, which are notoriously narcissistic (e.g., they are utterly self-absorbing and self-obsessive), moves against all tendencies towards self-centrism and self-aggrandizement; it represents "an appeal to a creative power with which the soul feels herself to be in connivance" (Gallagher, 1962, p. 74). This is why Marcel says that patience (including in the Baeckian sense) and humility are crucial aspects "of authentic hope, of hope which is at the same time trust and love (for these are not separable)". Baeck's for-the-other orientation was striking, indeed, throughout his ordeal he was other-directed, other-regarding and other-serving to his fellow Jews (and others) caught in the Nazi assault, both while living in Germany and in his incarceration in Theresienstadt.

Most importantly, perhaps, for Baeck, this patience was not only a question of "waiting" for relief, but had the additional element of "awaiting," (Pruyser, 1963, p. 89) for deliverance or salvation. That is, authentic hope requires a way of orienting oneself to the details and pragmatics of one's ordeal, to one's family and friends, with "*disponibilité*," Marcel's word for "availability," the capacity to let oneself be open and receptive to others, to be present, "a readiness of the self towards others and the world, as well as an involvement or engagement with the world" (Schrag, 2000, p. 1195). This includes allowing oneself to be helped by others, an important element in the inter-subjective context from which hope emanates. Such sensitive receptivity helps generate the conditions of possibility for creative, enlivening encounters between people, those other-directed, other-regarding and other-serving encounters that, says Marcel, can intimate transcendence. Humility, that quality of mind and heart of being modest and respectful to others and to things, is one of the important aspects of this dynamic availability, for it requires a renunciation of one's defensive, inordinate and infantile narcissistic investments that tend to block giving and receiving love from the people who are participating in your ordeal of suffering. "*Indisponibilité*," "unavailability," a kind of self-centric "holding back" and "closed-in-ness," (Cain, 1979, p. 65) is often expressed through pride, the haughty attitude of a person who believes, often unjustifiably, that they are better than others. For Marcel, the main characteristic of the prideful person is that he believes he is self-sufficient, a derivative of pathological narcissism that estranges oneself from meaningful encounters with others, from forms of "communion" with one's fellow human beings, as Marcel terms it: "Where pride reigns there is no room for mercy" [love]. (1973, p. 95). Hoping never judges another man's attitude towards his "reality," towards his ordeal of suffering, because the hoper knows that the nature of his "reality" is ever changing, ambiguous and indeterminate. Hoping, in other words, in part through its deference to doubt and uncertainty, always takes place in the context of reverence, of showing honor and respect to others (Pruyser, 1963, p. 90). Baeck's humility and respectfulness towards others was central to his way of being-in-the-world. Politeness and courtesy were his watchwords. As Baker (1978) noted, "And his courtesy—always jumping from his chair to greet visitors, holding their coats for them, accompanying visitors from his daughter's house to the bus top—became the source of many stories about him" (p. 332).

Another key aspect of hoping is that it has a strikingly different way of engaging time, one of the animating aspects of a person's view of reality. In contrast to a despairing or depressed person for whom time is experienced as "closed," like a "prison," the hoping person experiences time as "open" and "liberating." This is the prophetic nature of hope, says Marcel, who adds: "Of course one cannot say that hope sees what is going to happen; but it affirms as if it saw. One might say that it draws its authority from a hidden vision [including in the Baeckian sense] which it is allowed to take account without enjoying it" (1965, p. 53). Marcel continues, "if time is in its essence a separation and as it were a perpetual splitting up of the self in relation to itself, hope on the contrary aims at reunion, at recollection, at reconciliation; in that way, and in that way alone, it might be called a memory of the future." In other words, the despairing person feels the tight grip of the horror of the past, whereas the hoping person attempts to loosen its interpretive grip through imagining a better future, the difference between experiencing the world as a wall or as a gate. This is Baeck's historical imagination at work.

I have noted, following Marcel, that authentic hope is intimately connected to trust and love, always having an other-directed, other-regarding and other-serving thrust to it. More exactly, hope is never done in solitude as conventionally understood, rather it emanates from the inter-subjective context, always referring to the "we and the thou" (Keen, 1967, p. 43). Remember Baeck's caring and helpful relation to his flock while living in Nazi Germany and while imprisoned in Theresienstadt. Unlike desire, which is a more strictly narcissistic striving that anticipates the personal gratification of a particular wished-for thing, the hoping person requires others to flourish. Hope thus has an expansive, generous sweep to it, it hopes for everyone with whom the hoping person comes into contact.

Marcel famously captures the "for the other" nature of hope that is simultaneously thoroughly self-affirming when he writes, "I hope in thee for us" (1965, p. 60). The other, the "'Thou' is in some way the guarantee of the union which holds us together, myself to myself, or the one to the other, or these beings to those other beings." Hope, and the rise to communion that it entails, is the "glue" that keeps one together as a person amidst captivity. This appears to be the case for Baeck, as he noted, "Where men believe and love, they hope" (1964, p. 292).

Hoping, as I have suggested, is a constituent aspect of the existential structure of a human, it is fundamentally a centrifugal movement emanating from the deepest interior of a person, an other-directed, other-regarding, other-serving self-transcendent act of giving and receiving love. In fact, Marcel's most compelling and clear definition, given in the final six lines of his brilliant essay, "Sketch of a Phenomenology and a Metaphysic of Hope," beautifully suggests this point:

> We might say that hope is essentially the availability of a soul that has entered intimately enough into the experience of communion [the love relation] to accomplish in the teeth of will and knowledge the transcendental act [an act that is not restricted to what our desires are and what we reckon]—the act establishing the vital regeneration of which this experience both affords both the pledge and the first-fruits [the love relation is an experience already ours, and also an inkling of what could possibly be].
>
> *(Marcel, 1965, p. 67)*[21]

Hope thus requires a willing receptivity and engagement with others; in fact, it is this aspect of hoping that Marcel claims is its foundation: "there can be no hope which does not constitute itself through a *we* and for a *we*" (1973, p. 143). Baeck's kindly and helpful relationship to his community inside and outside of Theresienstadt comes to mind.

Most importantly, in Marcel's ontology it is this characteristic of hope that points to God. For Marcel, it is one's relationship to others, most directly and profoundly one's loving relationships, those animated by Goodness, Truth and Beauty, that are the "royal road" to the transcendent God. God, the Divine realm, can thus be conceptualized as "the 'Absolute Thou' who lurks in the truncated experience of presence felt as human communion" (Early and Gallagher, 2003, p. 134). Such a point of entry to the summoning God is not beyond everyday experience, but within it, what to the believer is embraced as moments of holiness (New World Encyclopedia (a)). "The way to heaven," Marcel warned, "is to dig down deep where you are" (Cain, 1979, p. 81). Said Baeck, "The way to our humanity does not lead away from our Judaism; it leads through our Judaism" (Friedlander, 1968, p. 35). Marcel spoke of the "ontological exigence," an impulse or urge that was the bedrock of the human condition, an irrepressible need, even a "demand" for the presence of being. Marcel's "being is an 'Absolute Thou,' not the whole of reality, a particular being, not being in general," but rather his God is an impulse to which we are mysteriously tied, "immanent in yet transcending our experience, to which we have access by the act we are at liberty to realize or not" (Rosthal, 1964, p. xii). It is, as I have said, by way of communion broadly described, that one's creatively pursues the Absolute Thou, a way of being that is also self-authenticating and the basis for one's self-presence (Pax, 1975, p. 20).[22] "Perpetual renewal," says Cain, "and continual self-intimacy" thus "go together" (Cain, 1995, p. 111). It is through the intimations of hoping and the cautious confidence regarding the future that it implies that is the surest testimony of the Godly, mysterious realm (Cooper, 1998). In a word, one becomes irrepressibly aware of the transcendent and bountiful nature of being, at its best.

While Baeck described his version of Judaism as a religion of optimism, I think this longing for deliverance or salvation, from the sword of the Egyptians and the waters of the Red Sea as it is recalled during Passover as it were, the fact is that Baeck appears to be more exactingly described as a hoping person than an optimist. Indeed, as Feller (2024) noted, despite the harsh conditions in Theresienstadt, and to a lesser extent while residing in Nazi Germany, "Baeck insisted that hope was possible in fact necessary" (p. 18). Feller continues,

> He made this point by contrasting the biblical prophets with the Western historiographical tradition, which he identified as espousing historical pessimism. Evil empires that thrived only on power and violent means, he comforted his audience in the ghetto would eventually collapse and be left in ruins. This for him was the message of the prophets in Theresienstadt.
>
> *(Feller, 2024)*

For Baeck then, it was the prophetic sensibility that greatly mattered to him. That is "Hebrew piety" as he called it, finds in its fulfillment not in a deliverance or salvation *from* the world, but in deliverance or salvation *in* the world, via the hallowing, making holy, of the world (Baeck, 1958, p. 53). "Both to be sent to the world by God and to expect his kingdom in the future is the essence of Jewish piety" (Baeck, 1948, p. 226). And again, "Piety means creating doorways through which the higher world enters into the finite, limited world" (Baeck, 1964 [1955], p. 210).

Conclusion

I have suggested that Baeck maintained the rudiments of his autonomy, integration and humanity, the basis of his goodness, through a number of interdependent, interrelated and interactive processes. Most importantly, it was his deeply internalized, strongly felt, flexibly and creatively applied, transcendent-pointing moral beliefs and values, that comprised his self, which potentiated in him the will and ability to sustain himself as a person. It was in part, via these considerations that Baeck was able to fend off personality disintegration. For example, Baeck was more adequately able to know, at least to some extent, how much of himself could be given to the state authorities while still protecting his flock and his own integrity. In this way he was better able to maintain a semblance of his "core" self, the self he knew before the Nazis came to power. I have also suggested that it was in the context of the existential trial of the Nazi assault, a form of captivity, enslavement and the temptation to despair, that Baeck was willing and able to maintain his hope ("hope is a response to tragedy"). Marcel viewed the basic form of dispositional hope as an open process, conveying human dignity as the aptitude to transcend one's own desires and to hope for a shared project (e.g., deliverance, salvation). Here hope transcends crude self-interest, it is other-directed, other-regarding and other-serving (Stratton-Lake, 1998). Marcel says that my relationship to the other person (or persons) in whom I have located my hope (e.g., fellow persecuted Jews and non-Jews) is not instrumental, but a collaborative, ethical relation of communion (e.g., "I hope in Thee for us"). Marcel understood such dispositional hope within the context of faith in the Absolute Thou (i.e., God), as well as obedience to God's commands to live a just, loving and humble life. Exactly how Baeck accomplished the aforementioned in the more extreme situation of Theresienstadt will be discussed in the next chapter.

Notes

1 I have in part, drawn from Marcus (1999, 2008, 2021) for this chapter and Chapter 3.
2 The notion of spiritual resistance has been criticized by some scholars alleging that it is a simplistic, redemptive narrative emanating from the postwar inability to reckon with the absence of meaning in mass murder (Hájková, 2020).
3 Neo-Kantian philosopher Hermann Cohen defines autonomy in an illuminating manner, in terms of self-legislation (the creation of laws by which one acts and lives); self-determination (self-creation); self-responsibility (taking responsibility for my own actions); self-preservation (the ultimate limit for the application of law) (Beiser, 2018).
4 Foucault describes this socio-intellectual reality as an episteme. Or put differently, episteme is the implicit presuppositions.
5 Baeck appears to have followed Ahad Ha-am's advice. Not to "follow the philosophers into the deep waters of metaphysics" (Noveck, 1963a, p. 31). Also worth mentioning is that like Buber, Baeck's emphasis is on the concrete and actual as opposed to the ideal and abstract (Friedman, 1963).
6 As Feller (2024) points out, Baeck viewed marriage as a "mystery and commandment," calling to mind the divine [*shekhina*] which sheltered the loving couple (p. 97). Baeck believed that such an I-Thou relationship culminated in giving birth to a child which was a form of revelation. Needless to say, Baeck was a family man, this being one of the "safe" places in reality or fantasy, amidst the Nazi assault (p. 98).
7 Survivors of the Holocaust will sometimes tell you that one of the worst humiliations upon arrival in Theresienstadt was to have to strip, let alone in front of those of the opposite sex, one's hair was cut short, and one was disinfected while one's clothes were fumigated (Hájková, 2020). One only can imagine how awful that was for a proud, 69 year-old rabbi like Baeck (assuming that he, along with the other inmates, were ordered to do so). Yet Baeck was deemed an "important functionary" and he might have avoided this humiliating ritual. Baeck also was given two rooms rather than one (allowing him more space), and he had his housekeeper with him (protecting him to some extent from the filth. She was also his secretary). Baeck also occasionally received some "care packages" while incarcerated (Baker, 1978).
8 In fact, at about the same time, Gandhi recommended "that the German Jews should engage in mass suicide, on a single day at a single hour, as a spectacular collective act of protest," to awaken Europe's conscience to their diabolical situation (Meyer, 2021, p. 128). Baeck rejected Gandhi's advice believing that the Jew must affirm life against all odds.
9 The prominent philosopher/translator Walter Kaufmann mentioned the "twofold" character of Baeck's writings in his anthology of Baeck's works (Kaufmann, 1981 [1958], p. 10). Twofoldedness refers to the tension of opposites which are integrated and united as a meaningful whole (Seligman, 1967).
10 Following the rabbinic teachings, Baeck believed that the Sabbath was the image of the messianic age (Friedlander, 1968). "The Sabbath, this 'sign of God' . . . is to be a reminder of both, of the meaning of the world as well as of the meaning of history, of the

cosmos as well as of freedom" (Baeck, 1964 [1955], p. 39). And again, "The Sabbath does not mean a mere not working, nor an empty idleness. It connotes something positive. It has guided the soul into its mystery so that it is not a day that just interrupts, but a day that renews, a day that has its own world" (Baeck, 1964 [1955], p. 137).

11 Tisha B'Av is an annual fast day in Judaism, commemorating a number of disasters in Jewish history.

12 At the time it was usual that the whole truth about a person having a terminal illness was withheld from them by doctors, the assumption being this was more humane.

13 Jewish functionaries prepared various propaganda events such as theatre plays that were meant to convince external inspectors of the humane treatment of the inmates within the ghetto (Hájková, 2020).

14 For Baeck, "freedom is the task which man is to fulfil and which he is able to fulfil because of the purity of his soul . . ." freedom "is the great commandment of man's life . . . freedom is the lifelong task of man – a task which makes it possible for him truly to live and to make his life a reality" (Baeck, 1948, p. 155).

15 Feller (2024), quoting Hájková, indicated that Baeck's housekeeper, Dora Czapski, was vital to much of Baeck's political and spiritual doings in Theresienstadt (and before that), sparing him at times from the inevitable exhaustion and lack of spare time. As Hájková notes, "Very few inmates of Theresienstadt were in a position to have a housekeeper" (2020, p. 51).

16 Unlike those who view prayer as dialogic, like Martin Buber and Franz Rosenzweig, Baeck viewed prayer as a monologue: "When a person speaks with God, it is in the highest sense of the word a monologue. . . . The person speaks, as it were, with the highest self, with the revelation of God that is within him. . . . In the highest sense he is speaking with himself" (Meyer, 2021, p. 204). As one survivor put it, there was "a genuine need to feel close to God in prayer" (Meyer, 2021, p. 150).

17 See Marcus (2013) for a psychoanalytically informed study of Gabriel Marcel, including his phenomenological study of hope.

18 Hope always has conscious, pre-conscious and unconscious aspects to it. As Erich Fromm (1968) points out, there are some individuals who feel consciously hopeful but may be unconsciously hopeless and others where it is the other way around.

19 For an illuminating discussion of the difference between hoping and optimism, see Montes (2023), and between hope and despair, see Healy (2023).

20 According to Meyer (pers. comm., 2024), optimism exists on this side of the abyss of evil while hoping exists beyond the abyss.

21 The parenthetical additions are drawn from Godfrey (1987, p. 235).

22 Marcel uses the term "Being" not only as a "God equivalent," he also uses it to signify a certain kind of "fullness," "being-as-fullness," as well as "that in which we are always grounded, that in which we always stand." Busch (1987, p. 35) further quotes Marcel as writing, in *Being and Having*, "We are involved in Being, and it is not within our power to leave it." (Marcel, 1965, p. 15).

3

SPIRITUAL RESISTANCE IN THERESIENSTADT

Baeck was described in a "nutshell" by H. G. Adler in the magisterial tome, *Theresienstadt 1941–1945. The Face of a Coerced Community* (2022 [1955]). According to Adler, himself a survivor of Theresienstadt who also knew Baeck, he had

> almost no enemies . . . he was well-respected among prisoners from many countries, and this respect increased due to his willingness to help others. He never isolated himself from the camp, yet it did not seem to exist in his presence . . . he could be gentle, but that was not the extent of his emotions; he could also show rage and scorn. He understood what was called for, and he was aware of the fateful failure to which the history subjected him and everybody else. It had bent him and thrown him into mourning, yet it did not break him, because he kept himself ready and open to fresh tasks in a spirit of tenacity and courage. He saw himself as a witness to the existence of another world beyond this fatal 'ghetto.'
>
> *(Adler, 2022 [1955], p. 215)*

Baeck was described as an "honorable example" of human decency, as "the conscience of the camp and was the focus of a moral resistance movement against the corruption and wretchedness of the Jewish leadership." He was "a beacon of light and a sea of tears in the midst of a surge of despair" (Adler, 2022 [1955]).

In this chapter I want to describe and explain how Baeck managed to maintain the rudiments of his autonomy, integration and humanity, the basis of his goodness, relatively speaking, amidst oppression in Theresienstadt. Compared to his former life in Germany, imprisonment in Theresienstadt was an existence within an environment of ever decreasing options and resources with which to sustain himself as a person.

DOI: 10.4324/9781003534327-3

Said Baeck after the war, "I was in Theresienstadt the number 187894. I had only this one thought: never to resign before rudeness, never to become a mere number, and always to keep my self-respect" (Baker, 1978, p. 3). This also applied to how he viewed other people saying, "We think too much in numbers. We forget that each man is a man with a soul and his body and his fear" (Baker, 1978, p. 227).

These quotations aptly describe Baeck's fundamental, existential orientation, his way of being-in-the-world while a prisoner in Theresienstadt. This is in keeping with Bruno Bettelheim's observation when he became imprisoned in the Dachau and Buchenwald concentration camps in 1938. Most importantly, said Bettelheim, what mattered most in terms of remaining human, was a will and ability to be approximately the same person he had been before being deprived of his freedom.

In Theresienstadt, the Nazi goal was to break the inmates as autonomous individuals, and to convert them into a passive and docile group from which no individual or group resistance could emerge. Adler referred to this as "massification" (2022 [1955], p. 595). The Nazis were totally committed to re-socializing the population, attempting to accomplish this task by systematically destroying individuality and dignity. In light of this systematized depersonalization amidst extreme conditions, Bettelheim writes that one of his main goals was "how to survive in ways that would protect my physical and moral existence" (Bettelheim, 1960, p. 13).

As so much of what Baeck accomplished by way of maintaining his autonomy, integration and humanity involved the "self," an illuminating definition of the self seems in order. The self as I apply it in this chapter are "webs of beliefs and desires, of sentential attitudes, webs which continually reweave themselves so as to accommodate new sentential attitudes" (Rorty, 1991, p. 93). Furthermore, according to Rorty, this web of belief stimulates the person into action, which produces new beliefs to be woven into the web, which in turn produces new actions, and so on, for as long as the person survives. In other words, "there is no self distinct from the self-weaving web. All there is to a human self is just that web" (Rorty, 1991, p. 93). For Baeck, it was his deeply internalized, strongly felt, flexibly and creatively applied, transcendent-pointing moral beliefs and values, that constituted the main foundation of his self: "the self is man's chosenness by God; it is therefore the chosenness of every man . . . it is his great ability to unfold through commandment and grace into an individual, a unique entity" (Baeck, 1964 [1955], p. 241). As Bettelheim notes about the self:

> What supports self-esteem and true independence is not fixed and unchanging, but depends on the vagaries of the environment. Each environment requires different mechanisms for safeguarding autonomy, those that are germane to success in living according to one's values in a particular environment.
>
> *(Bettelheim, 1960, p. 198)*

Anna Pawelczyńska, a sociologist and survivor of Auschwitz, elaborates Bettelheim's observation in a manner I think also applied to Baeck's experience in Theresienstadt, at least to some extent:

> Prisoners of Auschwitz had to be capable of creativity in the sphere of moral standards. . . . By reinterpreting the standards according to which they had been brought up and by practicing them in a necessarily diminished form, the prisoners were waging a battle on the moral plane with the most degenerate forms of power. Theirs was a battle in defense of those values to be saved under all circumstances.
>
> *(Pawelczyńska, 1979, pp. 140–141)*

What is pertinent for our understanding of Baeck in this discussion is the fact that in Theresienstadt what one did to support self-esteem was not fixed. As long as one had a relatively intact sense of self, that is, one's cherished beliefs and values, a wide range of behavior would have been necessary for an inmate to maintain his autonomy, integration and humanity in the changing, morally ambiguous circumstances of camp conditions. As Primo Levi noted, most inmates, most of the time, had to function amidst the "gray zone," a "zone of ambiguity which radiates out from regimes based on terror and obsequiousness" (Levi, 1986, p. 58). As Adler (2022 [1955]) indicated in his analysis of inmate behavior in Theresienstadt, there was "a demonic collapse of values," for example, the "the lapsed values of a bygone norm" (pp. 578, 581). For example, stealing bread from the communal kitchen was regarded as the "right" thing to do (even if in fact it may have meant less food for the other inmates) yet stealing bread from a fellow inmate was not. Quoting the Austrian writer Hermann Broch, Adler states that there was "decay of values" and "the values themselves were devalued" leading to extreme nihilism (2022 [1955], p. 564). As Bondy noted, "life in the ghetto [Theresienstadt] was full of the absurd: the performance of Verdi's *Requiem*, for example. Why, of all things, a Christian litany in a Jewish ghetto" (1980, p. 312).[1]

Such a decay of values was operative when we remember that Theresienstadt was not only a "model" ghetto constructed to deceive Red Cross inspectors and others (to verify that the Nazis were treating inmates humanely), but its actual character also constituted violence.[2] Theresienstadt was a transit camp for Auschwitz and other death camps which means that the typical inmate lived with the daily, pervasive and intense anxiety that they would be deported. To make matters even more diabolical, the deportation lists ordered by the Nazis were generated by the Jewish administration, a horrific undertaking. For how does one make such choices and still retain the rudiments of one's humanity?

From what I can discern, Baeck was not prone to this kind of downward modification of his moral outlook and behavior in the ghetto. As Deborah Dwork, author of *Children with a Star* (based on oral testimonies), makes a similar point about death and slave labor camps that I think to some extent also applies to life in Theresienstadt. Inmates,

> were in circumstances so narrowly constructed and so harshly imposed that it is difficult to conceive of any room for maneuver. And yet, everyone took decisions and made choices. They did not have the information they needed to make informed decisions and they were not at all certain what fate their choice would bring them.
>
> *(Dwork, 1991, p. 241)*

One important reason why it was so difficult for the inmate to make good decisions was because the Nazis constructed an environment in which the rationality of the prisoners was used to facilitate their own demise as autonomous, integrated and humane persons. Prisoners were constantly offered rational choices, almost always between evils, and in a system that was designed to completely operate against the inmate, every rational decision brought the inmate one step closer to self-destruction. As Bauman (1989) noted, "the rationality of the ruled is always the weapon of the rulers" (p. 142). Indeed, Baeck was criticized after the war for inadvertently doing the bidding of the Nazis, "cooperating," even though his intention, and that of other communal leaders, was to serve "their fellow Jews, not the Nazis, and to remain a center of resistance to Nazi rule" (Pasachoff, 1992, p. 151).

Such a horrendous context in which to make decisions brings Lawrence Langer's controversial notion of "choiceless choice" into sharp focus.[3] Choiceless choice refers to the fact that inmates "were plunged into a crisis . . . where crucial decisions did not reflect options between life and death, but one form of abnormal response and another, both imposed by a situation that was in no way of the victim's own choosing" (Langer, 1982, p. 72). For example, members of the Jewish Council had to decide who was to be deported and when, including sometimes separating family members.[4] In the death camps, an example of a choiceless choice was the fact that is some instances, a parent would have to choose which of their children would be given up to be gassed; or deciding whether to kill a newborn infant to save the mother, as giving birth was punishable by death to both mother and child.

Langer concludes that one cannot pass judgment on the moral behavior of inmates in situations where there is an absence of meaningful options. Moral choice, says Langer, had no meaning in Auschwitz and, he adds, it is impossible to relate such judgments to the inner freedom, morality or humanism celebrated by Bruno Bettelheim, Viktor E. Frankl and Terrence Des Pres and others.

Langer makes the important point that the death camp experience seems to demand a dramatic readjustment of the traditional notions of moral man, the linguistic categories that we conventionally use to understand behavior in extremity. And yet, I believe Langer is overstating his case and is mistaken in the main thrust of his argument. Surely, even amidst the excruciating moral dilemmas into which inmates were thrown, the principle remains the same: "a voluntary act performed for a consciously adopted reason and for another person implies a moral choice by a moral agent" (Angress, 1985, p. 188). As philosopher Edith Wyschogrod has concluded in another context, "Thus a single ethical act attests to the existence of an ethical field. While the camp system brutalized many, ethical acts emerge in the life-world in a 'ripple' effect which the camp system could not destroy" (Wyschogrod, 1988, p. 338). In a review of the survivor literature, Todorov makes a similar point:

> To put it simply, the most optimistic conclusion we can draw from life in (and outside) the camps is that evil is not unavoidable. The actual numbers are not important; what matters is that the possibility of choosing moral values continues to exist.
>
> *(Todorov, 1996, p. 41)*

Admittedly, the kinds of decisions that inmates had to make were affected by their greatly reduced freedom and limited options, but nevertheless, inmates made choices all along the way, at least in a limited sense, about how they were going to conduct themselves. To deny that inmates made meaningful choices, at least in certain contexts, is to deny their agency and to do this is to dehumanize the victim, something which is surely not Langer's intention, albeit a consequence of his formulation of the "choiceless choice." Indeed, as I indicate later in this chapter, the testimonials of Bruno Bettelheim, Primo Levi, Jean Améry, Viktor E. Frankl, Elie Wiesel, Anna Pawelczyńska (all Auschwitz survivors), H.G. Adler and Leo Baeck (Theresienstadt survivors) among others, that the central struggle for the inmate was the problem of "retaining one's humanity," implies that the inmates had meaningful moral choices to make throughout their ordeal of suffering (Bettelheim, 1960, p. 158).

Thus, what Baeck understood and personified was the fact he was a moral agent who had the capacity for making meaningful choices and decisions which aided him in his struggle to psychologically survive and remain human. Thus, as Adler noted, Baeck can be put in the category of those inmates who were willing and able to engage in "moral self-assertion," what he called, "kindhearted people."[5]

> The kindhearted were, as is the case everywhere in the world, the rarest and were found among all ages and groups: the Jews, and the baptized, the Zionists and the assimilated. They generally acted in silence, came without being called, and sacrificed themselves. They did what is in the nature of the kindhearted, which no outside circumstances can change and which has but one characteristic: kindness.
>
> *(Adler 2022 [1955], pp. 582, 593).*

The inmate's task of acting like an autonomous person was made more difficult in light of the fact that regardless of what modes of psychological or other protection one adopted in the concentration camp, in Theresienstadt, the bottom-line goal was the same, "to safeguard one's life." The fact that prisoner's lives were in such extreme peril most of the time, such as starvation and the threat of deportation, meant that there was little energy or interest left in personal integration and integrity for, "most of the time concern for personal integration and integrity had to be sacrificed to preserve life. . . . Most prisoners chose to be sure of their bread rather than their self-esteem" (Bettelheim, 1960, pp. 203–204). This being said, it was the maintenance of the subtle balance between satisfying individual needs and the demands of the camp environment that was continuously required.

Time and again, Bettelheim and others emphasize that the concentration camp inmates who were the best able to maintain their autonomy, integration and humanity were those who had a "consistent philosophy, either moral, political, or social [which] protected their integrity or gave them strength for an inner stand against Naziism" (Bettelheim, 1960, p. 120). Bettelheim believed that "an integrated personality and strong inner convictions, nourished by satisfying personal relations, [were] one's best protection against oppressive controls" (p. 105).[6] As Baeck noted, "He who has the inner conviction of possessing the truth, who lives for his religious ideal, must remain indifferent towards the successes of history, even though these may endure for centuries" (Baeck, 1948, p. 64). And again, "Only when a conviction has far-reaching greatness and its defenders are aware of its sublimity, is it heroic for man to live for it alone" (Baeck, 1948, p. 79).

> It is a well-known fact of the concentration camps that those who had a strong religious and moral conviction managed life there much better than the rest. Their beliefs, including belief in an afterlife, gave them a strength to endure which was far above that of most others. Deeply religious persons [like Baeck] often helped others, and some voluntarily sacrificed themselves—many more of them than of the average prisoners.
>
> *(Bettelheim, 1979, p. 296)*

Survivor testimony from the death camps supports Bettelheim's claim that transcending beliefs, values and moral convictions were critically important to concentration camps inmates in their struggle to maintain their autonomy, integration and humanity.

For example,

> The believers in any belief whatsoever, better resisted the seduction of power . . . they also endured the trials of the Lager [*Arbeitslager*, forced labor camp] and survived in proportionately higher numbers. . . . Not only during the crucial moments of selection or the aerial bombings but also in the grind of everyday life, the believers lived better.
>
> *(Levi, 1986, pp. 145–146)*

Jean Améry has noted that those inmates with strong beliefs or ideology had a "firm foothold in the world from which they spiritually unhinged the Nazi state" (Améry, 1980, p. 13). Elie Weisel has made a similar assertion:

> Within the system of the concentration camp . . . the first to give in, the first to collaborate—to save their lives—were the intellectuals, the liberals, the humanists, the professors of sociology, and the like. . . . Very few Communists gave in. . . . They were the resisters. . . . Even fewer to give in were the Catholic priests . . . yet there were exceptions. But you could not have found one single rabbi—I dare you—among all the *kapos* or among any of the others who held positions of power in the camps.[7]
>
> *(Wiesel, 1974, p. 273)*

Indeed, without such a transcendent belief/value structure the person is more likely to "fall[s] prey to the pressures of the state and to the fluctuations of worldly fortune." In other words, "models and values that are deeply internalized create the strength to resist every alien system which denies those values" (Pawelczyńska, 1979, p. 137). The aforementioned observations of Bettelheim, Levi, Améry, Weisel and Pawelczyńska are in sync with the insights of social theorists like Erving Goffman who wrote that "strong religious and political convictions have served to insulate the true believer against the assault of a total institution" (Goffman, 1961, p. 66).

Baeck appears to have been a "true believer," and understanding how these beliefs and values was enacted in Theresienstadt requires some illumination. This is especially important when we remember that beliefs and values are "successful rules for action" (Rorty, 1991, p. 65).

Baeck possessed, through his beliefs and values, a more or less coherent narrative of self-identity that gave him the ability to make sense of his suffering, gave direction to his life in Theresienstadt, and strengthened his autonomy, integration and humanity. This way of being-in-the-world was largely a traditional Jewish one (though he had a liberal take on tradition), one that was mainly, other-directed, other-regarding and other-serving. That is, while Baeck looked after his own needs and wishes (with some important assistance from his housekeeper) his main concern was to be a helper towards others. As Adler described the "helpers" in Theresienstadt, much of it applies to Baeck:

> They were realistic or optimistic and usually also active and strong willed. They grasped every situation, often had a sense of humor, and knew how to get their own way sufficiently. Where necessary, they took a hand in things and knew how to make something more or less out of nothing. They were good comrades, but not all of them were free of calculation, and thus some of them did not mind being compensated a little for their help; but they were basically agreeable and good natured. Many were invested with freshness and naivete, where some seemed rough. They were versatile and pliant by nature, and their company made daily life more bearable.
>
> *(Adler, 2022 [1955], pp. 592–593)*

The sociologist Anthony Giddens has noted that in general, it is through a narrative of self-identity that a person has the sense that he has biographical continuity which he is able to grasp reflexively and, to a greater or lesser extent, communicate to other people (Giddens, 1991, pp. 52–54). Baeck had decided that he would never surrender his self-respect and integrity as the earlier quotation indicates. In describing Theresienstadt, Adler notes that "Only within the areas of one's life into which terror could not intrude did true humanity assert itself. Externally, people became numbers, because power decided that it should be" (2022 [1955], p. 579). Baeck resisted, with all of his might, this structural aspect of the Nazi goal to make the inmate feel like an object. Rather, his kindhearted and helpful behavior in the ghetto gave him a feeling of moral agency, an assertion of his pre-incarceration sense of self.

A narrative, says Giddens, permits the person to have regular interaction with others in the day-to-day world and to integrate events which occur in the external world and sort them into the ongoing "story" about the self. Baeck's sense of self demanded that he live his religious consciousness in terms of engaging in other-directed, other-regarding and other-serving behavior. Baeck was, in terms of Adler's typology, was one of the kindhearted and helpful inmates. Moreover, says Giddens, a person with a more or less coherent narrative of self-identity is also more skillful at establishing a "protective cocoon," one that "filters out," in the practical conduct of everyday life, many of the dangers and primal anxieties which often threaten to undermine the integrity of the self. Such a person has a more securely anchored sense of ontological security. As Baeck noted,

> The life of a man can and should be more than just a sequence of days more than a fate that has to come to be and is coming to be. When man chooses his life, when he makes it the task which God sets for him, the commandment that God has given him; then even amidst the flux of the immediate, his life will have its share of what is coming to be. . . . A life goes astray when it does not find the possibilities which are innate in it. A life fulfills itself when it understands and accepts that which is sent to it.
>
> *(Baker, 1978, p. 167)*

As Baker points out, the aforementioned was the rationale that Baeck gave to become the president of the *Reichsvertretung*[8] while living in Germany, however, I believe that this outlook was to some extent also operative in the daily struggle in Theresienstadt.

Finally, as Giddens suggests, through a narrative of self-identity the person is better able to accept that integrity as worthwhile. There is adequate self-esteem, self-continuity and self-coherence to sustain a sense of the self as "alive," within the scope of reflexive control, rather than having the inert quality of things in the object world. Massification was an attempt to make the ghetto inmate feel like inhuman, a mere number. However, through a coherent narrative of self-identity Baeck was able to feel a greater sense of personality integration and personhood. This was in part, because he was less overwhelmed by the Nazi assault, because he was able to test the vast number of choices which had to be made in the ghetto against his beliefs and values and interests, and thereby reduced the wide range of problems to a manageable size. In other words, Baeck felt less overpowered than other inmates by any need for decisions in judging how much of himself he could surrender to the Nazi system and still maintain his autonomy, integration and humanity (Bettelheim, 1960).

Bettelheim claims that the inmate needed to hold on "with utter tenacity" to the "essential convictions" that became the foundation for his resistance to Nazi inhumanity (Bettelheim, 1960, p. 157). For Baeck, these essential convictions were his transcendent-pointing moral beliefs and values. Moreover, says Bettelheim, with regards to these "essential convictions" "one had to keep oneself informed at all times" because they were the foundation of one's humanity. For Bettelheim, and this applies to Baeck too, an awareness of one's attitude toward compliance to Nazi demands was crucial throughout one's ordeal of suffering.

> This keeping informed and aware of one's actions—though it could not alter the required act, save in extremities—this minimal distance from one's own behavior, and the freedom to feel differently about it depending on its character (which) . . . permitted the prisoner to remain a human being. It was giving up all feelings, all inner reservations about one's actions, the letting go of a point at which one would hold fast no matter what, that changed prisoner into a Moslem [one of 'the walking dead'].
>
> *(Bettelheim, 1960, p. 158)*

Baeck possessed an "inner power of resistance" based on the attitudinal freedom that he cultivated. He had "a personality capable of and meant for autonomy" (Adler, 2022 [1955], p. 560). He was,

> unerringly aware of the weakness and corruption of his environment, which he attempted to counteract as best he could, first and foremost through his honorable example . . . he guarded the gates behind which even greater evils loomed, and no one could push aside.
>
> *(Adler, 2022 [1955], p. 215).*

My point is that Baeck creatively used his traditional Jewish outlook as a moral resource to guide him in his autonomous actions. That is, he realized that:

> However restrictive an oppressive environment may be, even then the individual still retains the freedom to evaluate it. On the basis of this evaluation he is also free to decide on his inner approval or resistance to what is forced upon him.
>
> *(Bettelheim, 1960, p. 69)*

It was a capacity to choose his response towards his ordeal of suffering, that allowed him to retain his humanity and perhaps even life itself (Bettelheim, 1960, pp. 158–159). Such an independence of mind was crucial to retain one's humanity, especially when we remember that "every day, every hour, offered the opportunity to make a decision, a decision which determined whether you would or would not submit to those powers which threatened to rob you of your very self, your inner freedom" (Frankl, 1963, p. 104).[9] Baeck used his agency, such as his decision-making capacity to shield himself from the worst aspects of the Nazi regime. Moreover, he was able to use a narrative in which he understood his compliance to the Nazis, not as absolute capitulation and degradation, but rather as a necessary strategic compromise in order to survive. As a result, he still retained a sense of himself as the same person he was prior to his imprisonment. As Pawelczyńska (1979) pointed out, "He who under conditions of terror and coercion achieved inner freedom, at least to some extent, carried off the only form of victory possible within the existing situation" (p. 141).

Inmates like Baeck had a more-or-less coherent narrative of self-identity that provided direction to their lives in Theresienstadt. Baeck and other likeminded inmates were less likely to violate their basic moral sense of themselves and could avoid feeling destructive negative emotions to what they would regard as objectionable behavior (e.g., they felt less guilt and shame). What Bettelheim observed probably also applied to Baeck:

> To survive as a man not a walking corpse, as a debased and degraded but still human being, one had first and foremost to remain informed and aware of what made up one's personal point of no return, that point beyond which one would never, under any circumstances, give in to the oppressor, even if it meant risking and losing one's life. It meant being aware that if one survived at the price of overreaching this point one would be holding on to a life that had lost all its meaning. It would mean surviving—not with a lowered self-respect, but without any.
>
> *(Bettelheim, 1979, p. 284)*

Bettelheim also notes that an inmate had to keep himself informed of how he felt about complying when the ultimate decision as to where to stand firm was *not* called into question. These are the decisions that related to situations that did not challenge the inmate's main beliefs and values, his essential convictions, and did not bring about a sense of degradation and demoralization if violated. Such decisions were on the periphery of the inmate's belief/value system. Bettelheim stresses the point, that to some extent, for all inmates to survive they had to comply with authority:

> One had to comply with many of the debasing and amoral commands if one wished to survive; but one had to remain cognizant that one's reasons for complying was 'to remain alive and unchanged as a person.' Therefore, one had to decide, for any given action, whether it was truly necessary for one's safety or that of others, and whether committing it was good, neutral or bad.
>
> *(Bettelheim, 1960, p. 158).*

For Baeck to survive at the expense of his essential convictions, his cherished beliefs and values, would mean to violate his very sense of his self, an experience that would quite likely generate intense guilt and a feeling of humiliation, which would make it impossible for Baeck to embrace himself as anything like the person he was prior to his ordeal of suffering. For Bettelheim, and probably for Baeck, it is precisely this capacity to feel genuine guilt that helped him to retain his humanity, however, if this guilt was too deep and pervasive it could lead to debilitating humiliation, despair and loss of motivation to struggle to survive. By humiliation I mean, following Rorty (1989), that when the narrative that a person has been telling himself about his life has been rendered almost completely meaningless, it cuts deeply into his motivation to carry on.

For Baeck, this kind of attack on the coherence of his narrative of self-identity would have been unbearable. Such a humiliating narcissistic shock would foster intense feelings of apathy, resignation and despair. Most importantly perhaps, such subversion of identity would undermine Baeck's sense of ontological security, that all-important sense of continuity and order of events. As Giddens points out, when one's ontological security is severely assaulted, chaos breaks in, but "this chaos is not just disorganization, but the loss of a sense of the very reality of things and of other persons" (Giddens, 1991, p. 36). Said Baeck, his ghetto experience "officially ousted his name and it threatened inwardly to oust his self."

> That was the mental fight everyone had to keep up, to see in himself and in his fellow man not only a transport number. It was the fight for the name, one's own and the other's, the fight for individuality, the secret being, one's own and the other's, the fight for individuality. Much, perhaps everything, depended on whether one stood the test, that the individual in one remained alive as an individual and continued to recognize the individual in the other.
>
> *(Baker, 1978, p. 287)*

Baeck, like Bettelheim and many other survivors was referring to the will and ability to maintain one's autonomy, integration, and most importantly, one's humanity amidst the onslaught. That is, to protect himself from dehumanization induced by, for example, the anonymity of a number, filth, hunger, lack of space, fear and so forth. This, said Baeck, was "the fight . . . for the individual day."

(Baker, 1978, p. 288)

Theresienstadt, constructed purposely in order to deceive, distract and divert outside attention from humanitarian organizations, was an "inverted world" (Katz, 2014, p. 168),

> a uniquely illusory world, where few could distinguish between reality and deception . . . every characteristic, and every trait had lost or changed its original meaning . . . people were confused, were made confused, and even confused the confusion.
>
> *(Adler, 2022 [1955], pp. 586, 587)*

Indeed, to survive such a psychotic-like environment as Adler describes it, required a degree of "split consciousness" (Adler, 2022 [1955], p. 586), simply defined as a defense mechanism in which the individual fails to integrate positive and negative experiences of oneself and others. Perceiving matters as "all good" or "all bad" is the watchword of splitting (Bettelheim, 1960).[10]

Splitting was a process in which the inmate generated a "split" in his personality between the inner self that might be able to retain its integrity, and the rest of the personality that would have to submit and adjust for survival. Inmates framed what was happening to them as if "These dreadful and degrading experiences were somehow not happening to 'me' as a subject, but only to 'me' as an object," which permitted them to feel that their pre-incarceration self-identity was largely unchanged amidst a violent and radically changing and uncertain external world (Bettelheim, 1960, p. 127). Many inmates felt detached, "as if what happened did not really matter to oneself" (Bettelheim, 1960, p. 127). It is unclear whether Baeck did much splitting in Theresienstadt, although, "He never isolated himself from the camp, yet it did not seem to exist in his presence" (Adler 2022 [1955], p. 215). Likewise, Baker (1978) reports a fellow inmate's words, "Leo Baeck was untouched by Theresienstadt. He never was really there" (p. 287). That is, he was there for others, but he was not there in that he was not significantly touched by his hostile environment (Meyer, 2024).

Pingel (1991), presents an alternative explanation to the issue of splitting that may apply to Baeck. Baeck may have altered his behavior only to the extent that was absolutely necessary in the ghetto. Inmates, of course, had a highly restricted code of judgment and latitude for action at their disposal, and accepted, at least temporarily, that this condition would have to suffice throughout their ordeal of suffering. "Selective apathy" and "active denial" of portions of ghetto reality, such as not allowing oneself to be overwhelmed by starvation, illness (e.g., typhus, enteritis), despair and death, was necessary (e.g., public executions). Such emotional blocking was crucial to endure the everyday tribulations in the ghetto but was not necessarily operative in helping to maintain an inmate's sense of his pre-incarceration personality core as is assumed in Bettelheim's formulation of splitting.

In the following section I want describe how Baeck, qua traditional Jew (with liberal leanings), used his "Jewish" resources to help maintain his autonomy, integration and humanity. For one must remember that above all else, Baeck viewed himself as a rabbi, a teacher and scholar, and he consciously and unconsciously drew from this outlook and behavior to make his suffering "sufferable."

Self-Transcendence in Therseinstadt

To quote Auschwitz survivor/author, Jean Améry:

> Whoever is in the broadest sense, a believing person, whether his belief be metaphysical [e.g., devout Jews and Catholics, Jehovah Witnesses) or bound

> to concrete reality [e.g., Marxists, political Zionists], transcends himself. He is not captive of his individuality; rather he is part of a spiritual continuity that is interrupted nowhere, not even Auschwitz.
>
> *(Améry, 1980, p. 14)*

Moreover,

> One way or the other, in the decisive moments their political or religious belief was an inestimable help to them, while we skeptical and humanistic intellectuals took recourse, in vain, to our literary, philosophical, and artistic household gods. Their belief or their ideology gave them the firm foothold in the world from which they spiritually unhinged the SS state. Under conditions that defy the imagination they conducted Mass, and as Orthodox Jews they fasted on the Day of Atonement although they actually lived the entire year in a condition of raging hunger. They survived better or died with more dignity than their irreligious or intellectual comrades, who often were infinitely better educated and more practiced in exact thinking.
>
> *(Améry, 1980, p. 13)*

As I have suggested, Baeck had a religious consciousness (Borowitz, 1983), one that resonates with Améry's observations. That is, he had self-transcending beliefs and values lodged in a passionately felt, direct relation to God. This included a God-inspired devotion and worship, and perhaps even more importantly, in Baeck's outlook, God commanded ethical conduct, responsibility to the other, as prescribed in for example, sacred texts like the Talmud. Moreover, Baeck's suffering, and the devout Jew's suffering in general, was to be understood and responded to in terms of his love and awe of God, who was characterized by inexhaustible mystery/commandment, sacredness, radical alterity, compassion and justice. This point was expressed by the Hasidic Rabbi Levi Yitzhak of Berditchev, whose words probably convey this animating feature of Baeck's and the devout Jew's capacity to make his suffering sufferable via his heartfelt, dialogic relation to the Eternal One:

> Master of the universe. I do not know what questions to ask. I do not expect You to reveal Your secrets to me. All I ask is that You show me one thing—what this moment means to me and what You demand of me. I do not ask why I suffer. I ask only this: Do I suffer for Your sake?
>
> *(Rabinowicz, 1982, p. 94)*

For a devout Jew like Baeck, at the deepest level of the self, God was an intimate presence, an exemplary other, a partner in the never-to-be finished work of creation and *tikkun olam* (repairing the world). Though at times God was experienced as enigmatic and ambiguous, a mystery as Baeck would say, He participated in the pain and suffering of His creatures, of Israel and of individual Jews. This partnership in suffering, in which God is concerned and implicated in the fate of His people, is injured by their pain and suffering, and liberated by their redemption, in part, constituted the divine pathos from which the devout Baeck experienced, understood and to some extent, transcended his particular suffering (Wolf, 2004, pp. 303–304).

What Baeck, qua traditional Jew, appeared to have is the symbolic capacity to place proximate acts in ultimate meaning-giving, affect-integrating, action-guiding contexts and in so doing, decisively altered the Nazi landscape. Devout Jews like Baeck viewed Nazi brutality against the background of other Jewish calamities which, while it does not adequately explain the Nazi brutality, it does at least place it in an actionable moral, cognitive and affective context. The devout Jew's beliefs and values tended to render their experience intelligible and within cognitive understanding. The point is that inmates like Baeck, mainly through their meaning-giving, affect-integrating and action-guiding relationship with God "transcended themselves and projected themselves into the future. They were no windowless monads; they stood open, wide open onto a world that was not the world of Auschwitz" or Theresienstadt (Améry, 1980, p. 14). As Baeck noted, the ancient Rabbis had the living conviction that they had been called on by God. "He who is conscious of such a call feels that he has been sent to the future, and he is therefore able to wait for and appeal to the future" (Baeck, 1958, p. 61).Put differently, this is a "positon of readiness, to be prepared for the future without having a map of the future (Katz, 2014, p. 92).

What Baeck had, at least to some extent, was the capacity to lose himself in a transcending symbolic world. Without such a symbolic world, terror is overwhelming. A symbolic world is roughly equivalent to a perspective, "a particular manner of construing the world" (Geertz, 1973, p. 16). Religion, politics and psychoanalysis can act as a symbolic world. For example, a religious Jew like Baeck could draw some comfort from the doctrine of *Kiddush Hashem*, the sanctification of the Divine Name, often through martyrdom.[11] Says Baeck,

> Martyrdom is the truest sanctification of the Holy Name, the clearest testimony of God, the most certain proof of God's existence. It is the final word, the ultimate consequence of moral responsibility. Where there is the unconditional duty to testify of God through faith in Him and obedience to His imperatives, the boundary of our existence is not the boundary of our duty. Our life is little and poor against the exaltedness and fullness of the task. The finest life means nothing compared to the moral demand. And thus we must be ready to sacrifice our life for the good. The ethical will finds its sole goal in its agreeing with God. And to agree with God, man must be able *to surrender his will for life.*
>
> *(Friedlander, 1968, p. 87)*

What Baeck is saying here is that death is not the final word of the ethical imperative. The ethical drive had an "unyieldingness" of Israel's stubborn faith. Israel, and the individual Jew must be willing and able to suffer for his faith (Friedlander, 1968, p. 88). According to Baeck,

> in martyrdom death is no longer a mere end of life, a mere fate. It becomes a deed of freedom and love for God . . . death becomes in martyrdom a proof of that power, a proof of man's freedom. Through his death the martyr gives reality to the commandment; as the old saying puts it, he creates himself through death.
>
> *(Baeck, 1948, p. 174)*

Kiddush Hashem, as Baeck views it, was thus a notion and behavioral instruction that acted as a guide for Jewish responses to crisis and catastrophe (Huberband et al., 1987). In Theresienstadt, and certainly in the death camps, the belief that one's death in some way sanctified God served to diminish the death panic by giving an other-worldly meaning and focus to his or her death. The belief that he would be rewarded in the world-to-come for his sacrifice, and there would be some kind of divine retribution against the Nazi enemies, reassured and comforted the devout Jew like Baeck in the face of death. In a certain sense, religious Jews like Baeck did not feel that they were passive victims in the face of persecution. They did not wish to die, but their capacity to interpret their death as a holy act of Kiddush Hashem, as the ultimate expression of their responsibility to their beloved God, indicates a choice and action. Such inmates were able to will meaning into their suffering and death. By anchoring their identity in a cosmic reality, religious inmates like Baeck were, to some extent, protected from the terror associated with anticipating and facing death. As Montefiore (1958) noted, "The Jewish faith that supported and sustained the martyrs of old, from Rabbi Akiba onwards, illuminated Baeck himself" (1958, p. 7).

Maintaining a Degree of Dignity and Self-respect

As noted earlier, non-religious and non-political inmates were more vulnerable to the Nazi assault than religously devout and political inmates (though there were important differences between the two groups (Marcus, 1999). Their self-esteem had heavily relied on a status and respect that came with their positions, depended on their occupations, on being head of a family, or similar external factors.

The radical loss of self-respect played havoc with inmates in relation to both their former social status and to their sense of personal worth. While all persons require a degree of affirmation by the social world, for Baeck who had an eastern European sensibility, and for other religious inmates, what mattered most was what kind of Jew one is. As the theologian Eliezer Berkovits says, for Eastern European Jews, "Ultimately, what really matters is what kind of Jew one is, that alone is the source of one's self-respect" (Berkovits, 1979, p. 55). Baeck had a similar perpective when he said "Jewish existence" was never "existence for itself. . . . The Jew lives before God, not in God. . . . The Jew lives before

God. Before God. And therefore he is ultimately risen above the surrounding" and "led away from danger" (Feller, 2024, p. 92). As Meyer (2021, p. 148) noted, in Theresienstadt Baeck engaged in an "ongoing struggle to remain, at least in his own eyes, more than a number, never to capitulate to the filthy surroundings, and always to safeguard his self-respect." Baeck wanted to survive like any other inmate, but not at any cost, that is, not at the cost of betraying the meaning of his own life (Berkovits, 1979).

To the extent that the devout Jew lived a life based on his "core" Jewish beliefs and values of responsibility, to God and tradition, the Jewish people, and to his fellow human beings, he regarded himself worthwhile, dignified and deserving of God's blessing in this world or the world to come. The point is, that Baeck, qua religious Jew relied less on the external world, he was more rooted inside himself, in a realm of the spirit that was less vulnerable to the uncertain destiny of an outside reality (Berkovits, 1979, p. 54). Baeck was better able to sustain himself as a person because, in his view, he did not fashion his identity mainly from the values and standards of the Christian, capitalist, Western society that was devouring them (Berkovits, 1979, p. 54). In Theresienstadt, "an individual could preserve his personality only in the parts of his life where even this power [Nazi coercion] could not penetrate, at least until the moment of physical murder" (Adler, 2022 [1955] p. 578). To accomplish the aforementioned required the will and ability to fend off the "fear and misery" and "decayed morality" that constituted the ghetto environment (Adler, 2022 [1955], p. 593). As Baeck said, "All true faith is a faith that raises itself above fate: it is the will that springs up within this faith, the will to fashion and to create, to fulfill the moral law" (Meyer, 2021, p. 94).

As Meyer explains:

> Baeck's writings in the early Nazi period argued for a particular posture that he called *Haltung or Zuruckhaltung*. By the former, he meant a composed stance, a self-determination that did not allow the oppressor to undermine self-image or self-esteem. It was the antidote to fate.
>
> *(Meyer, 2021, p. 103)*

It was in part, through *Haltung*, that you displayed self-control and therebye sustained your dignity. *Zuruckhaltung* was "holding back," that is, not permitting unwieldly emotions to determine your outlook and behavior, "not getting swept away," this being the precondition of *Haltung* (Meyer, 2021, p. 103). In 1934, Baeck wrote:

> When a person is struck by fate, he retains one thing that enables him to confront fate: *Haltung*. . . . True *Haltung* is always the revelation of a spiritual possession it is the expression of an inner solidity and dignity.
>
> *(Meyer, 2021)*

Thus, Baeck resided in a different realm of the spirit. He appears to have what he called a "pious heart." A pious heart, Baeck declares, "knows what is real and what is the basis of all life." That is, "in all that is transitory he sees the eternal, in all that is of earth he sees the infinite, in all that lives he sees the presence of God." In this way he says, "the world and his own life are eloquent with messages of revelation" (Baeck, 1958, p. 32).

Membership of a Group

As Adler noted about Baeck in Theresienstadt, "Baeck embodied the conscience of the camp and was the focus of a moral reistance movement against the corruption and wretchedness of the Jewish leadership" (2022 [1955], p. 215). Said Baeck,

> People who had not known each other endeavored to help each other, physically and spiritually. They gave each other of whatever they had, of their belongings and of their spirit. Human beings found each other, and where the individual held on to himself, there also arose a community.
>
> *(Baker, 1978, p. 295)*

Indeed Baeck probably viewed himself as a member of a sub-community of Jewish religous inmates, a crucial source of emotional sustenance, morale building and practical help to its members. The fact that Baeck lectured to the inmate community, and facilitated discussion groups (Feller, 2024) often on Jewish themes, meant that he was able to affirm his Jewishness and scholarship, that is, his pre-incarceration self. An island of freedom as I mentioned earlier. This being said, as Adler indicates, for the most part:

> People rarely used genuinely Jewish ways of thinking to contemplate the problem of general humanity. Despite the influence of Leo Baeck and some others, it appeared that few people had any use for Judaism that was not combined with the cheap tools of an ideology—that is, something fundamentally alien to Judaism.
>
> *(Adler, 2022 [1955], p. 597)*

Thus, the community, or at least part of the ghetto community, offered Baeck a socially supportive context to sustain his counternarrative to the dehumanizing Nazi reality. He may have been able to recreate, usually in a modified form, aspects of his former community, such as prayer and study that Baeck said enhanced individual freedom in Theresienstadt, and in other camps, these likeminded inmates tended to stay together and help one another.

As the Auschwitz survivor/psychoanalyst Anna Ornstein noted, "the creation of small groups provided an opportunity to experience and express aspects of the nuclear self, specifically related to the pole of ideals, and it provided the all-important empathic selfobject[12] matrix that reinforced a modicum of self esteem" (Ornstein, 1985, p. 115).

Moreover, Todorov points out, with regards to concentration and death camps, group membership, while almost always a helpful resource, was a morally ambiguous issue. For example, it could mean that a group member automatically helps all of the members of his group and does not concern himself with the needs of those who do not belong. The Communists, for example, fashioned insular groups "from which all those who did not share their convictions were excluded." Moreover, unlike religious believers, an enemy of the Communists, say a *kapo* or Nazi informer, would in some instances be killed by a group member. The Jehovah's Witnesses were the most tightly knit group, their love for Jehovah being so passionate that they refused all accommodation and compromise with the Nazis. However, according to Todorov, none of their fellow prisoners benefited from that love. He quotes Ravensbrück survivor Margarete Buber-Neumann, "If they took any risks at all, it was only in the service of Jehovah—and never of their fellow prisoners" (Todorov, 1996, pp. 57–58).

In fact, as Baker (1978) points out "there were religious observances at Theresienstadt."[13] Moreover, he reports that "many attended services [e.g., on the Sabbath] conducted by their own rabbis—the Berlin Jews usually attended Baeck's" (p. 302). In addition, says Baker, there were community seders held to celebrate Passover, commemorating the Jews' exodus from slavery in Egypt (i.e., a story of slavery, freedom and redemption). The important symbol of matzah was typically supplied by the Red Cross or other organizations outside Europe. For the holiday of Purim, "the Jews at Theresienstadt had a Megillah Esther, a scroll telling the story of how Esther and Mordechai saved the Jews from destruction by Haman, which they read during the service" (Baker, 1978, p. 303). Finally, of the "many services conducted in Theresienstadt" the Bar Mitzvah were the most impressive. In these celebrations the Jews reaffirmed their commitment to pass on their religion and their life to their children (Baker, 1978, p. 303). Similarly, Baeck officiated at weddings and funerals[14] that had a degree of symbolic significance in terms of Jewish continuity and hope.

There were also religious services for the many Protestants and Catholics in Theresienstadt, that is, those whom the Nazi's believed had Jewish lineage (i.e., a Jewish parent or grandparent) even though they did not view themselves as Jews and throughout their lives lived as Christians. "Many of the Christians knew and liked Baeck," in fact one Catholic indicated that Baeck did not benefit from his position of power as did some of the other officials. Moreover, Baeck "was a link between those of different religions and ideas. We Catholics honored him especially, and he was a frequent guest at our meetings . . . respect and tolerance for the fellow man formed the basis of his ethics" (Baker, 1978, pp. 302–303).

Baeck also supported "lay Catholics conducting marriage ceremonies" (Feller, 2024, p. 133), claiming that if he could show Christians kindness he would be fulfilling the larger function of being emotionally present, qua Jew, for those in need. In other words, Baeck's kindness was not limited to Jews.

It would appear that Baeck viewed himself as having a spiritual membership of a community, that theoretically at least, had existed for thousands of years and was inspired by thoughts of contact with the Eternal God. Such membership for Baeck, and other devout Jews, was mainly brought about through living a life, even in Theresienstadt, of relative selflessness, compassion and justice. As Baeck noted in another context, "He realizes that he does not stand alone either in space or time, and his fellowship with others is a constant source of strength, assurance and confidence." Moreover, "He becomes still more conscious of all this when the existence of the community takes on in his mind the Messianic, world-wide meaning, and thus seems to guarantee to him, individual though he be, a place in history" (Baeck, 1958, p. 71). Baeck was "a beacon of light and a sea of tears in the midst of a surge of despair" (Adler, 2022 [1955], p. 215).

It is worth remembering that the aforementioned religious observance was not only in Theresienstadt. In addition, it has been reported that in concentration and death camps, devout Jews participated in communal religious rituals such as secretly praying together, observing the Sabbath and the holidays, lighting Hanukkah candles, keeping kosher, studying the Torah, baking matzahs, and "conducting" Passover seders (Landes, 1983a, 1983b). Some Hasidim in Bergen-Belsen even made a *sukkah* (a hut in which observant Jews reside during the seven-day festival of Sukkot, commemorating God's providence over the Israelites in the desert). Straw from a torn and dirty mattress acted as a makeshift roof (Elliach, 1980). For the devout Jew, the community was considered to have intrinsic spiritual value and meaning. The preservation of "mitzvah-based communities" (Landes, 1983a, p. 265) was a way of maintaining and expressing the Jew's deeply internalized beliefs and values, which gave individual Jews the feeling that their pre-incarceration sense of self was not completely extinguished. Religious observances, truncated as they may have been, offered the vision of a better reality that gave inmates the strength to press on. Religious observances also generated lines to personal past memories and future hopes so that the present was tolerable (Landes, 1983a, p. 265). Finally, religious observances aided the inmate's survival as it tended to help them reconstitute their ontological security thereby defending themselves against the Nazi attempts at dehumanization and depersonalization.

While I stress the "positive" aspects of the believer's mode of being, I am aware that the matter is extremely complex. For example, in certain instances, maintaining a strong religious conviction could diminish an inmate's chances of personal survival as well as threaten the lives of fellow inmates. Langer tells of a group of Hasidim who declined to work in a brush factory on Yom Kippur, deciding instead to pray. Other inmates "pleaded with them, fearing for their own safety if the Germans discovered that the output was less than expected." The Hasidim however, refused. The SS became aware of the situation and shot the Hasidim, "and began beating and randomly executing some of the other inmates" (Langer, 1982, pp. 70–71).

Finally, it should be mentioned that in some instances engaging in certain intellectual activity such as remembering or discussing a poem, helped an inmate remain human by providing him with a "tiny island of freedom" and "a moment of spiritual transcendence" (Todorov, 1996, p. 93). Moreover, some inmates were able to sustain aspects of their humanity and continue to struggle to survive by virtue of moral convictions that were not lodged in religious or political transcending ideologies, such as devotion to a wife or child they hoped to see again, or "bearing witness" for the sake of future generations. In Baeck's case, his lecturing on secular philosophers and the like, and engaging in discussion groups probably had the aforementioned function. The fact that his daughter, son-in-law and grandchild were safe in London probably was another reason to fight for survival.

Sustaining Himself as a Person in Theresienstadt

Baeck, qua devout Jew, had a symbolically mediated relation between himself and the death world of Theresienstadt that gave him a specific meaning to his environment in the ghetto, one that was "symbolic of a transcendent" truth (Geertz, 1973, p. 98), that gave him a more helpful general orientation through which to view the horror he was experiencing. As Baeck noted about Theresienstadt:

> More and more people were crammed into a small, ever shrinking space, so that each person was constantly bumping into and rubbing up against everyone else;[15] as intended, all manner of selfishness and greed blossomed, and all decency withered away . . . the realm of life was replaced by the realm of death.
>
> *(Baeck, 2022 [1955], p. xi)*

This aforementioned self-sustaining transcendent truth was rooted in a deep-seated sense of a God-emanating responsibility for the other (Baeck's "commandment"), a truth that to some extent, made Baeck steadfast and immovable, maybe even serene, relatively speaking. For a devout Jew like Baeck, the extreme situation of the ghetto and camps had a greater degree of "interpretability" (Geertz, 1973, p. 100). That is, Baeck did not feel utterly overwhelmed by a situation that was "at the limits of . . . [his] analytic capacities, at the limits of . . . [his] powers of endurance, and at the limits of . . . [his] moral insight" (Geertz, 1973). Geertz further says, if situations of "bafflement, suffering, and a sense of intractable ethical paradox" become intense enough or are endured long enough, they radically challenge people's ability to orient themselves effectively within them. Such situations threaten "to unhinge" one's mind (Geertz, 1973). Baeck was probably not as vulnerable to such toxic elements of the ghetto environment: "Without faith, without a religious philosophy to sustain us, we would have found it impossible to maintain our sanity" (Feller, 2024, p. 134).

What Baeck had could be roughly described as symbolic resources to make the extreme situation "sufferable." Similar to other devout Jews, he had religious symbols which provided "a cosmic guarantee not only for . . . [his] ability to comprehend the world, but also, comprehending it, to give a precision to . . . [his]feeling, a definition to . . . [his] emotions" that enabled him to better endure the extreme situation. Intense, relentless brute pain could be endured "by placing it in a meaningful context, providing a mode of action through which it can be expressed, being expressed understood, and being understood, endured" (Geertz, 1973, pp. 104, 105).

It should be emphasized that Theresienstadt was not only a situation to be suffered, it also threatened the inmates' ability to engage in moral judgments. The ghetto challenged the individual's means to generate a real-world set of ethical criteria, normative standards to steer their actions in the face of extreme evil, suffering and death (Geertz, 1973, p. 106). As Levinas points out, evil is both "inside" suffering and a notion we use to evoke it: "the evil of pain, the deleterious per se, is the outburst and deepest expression, so to speak, of absurdity." That is, "the least one can say about suffering is that, in its own phenomenality, intrinsically, it is useless: 'for nothing.'" (Levinas, 1998, p. 93). As pointed out earlier, Baeck had to make some very difficult moral decisions in the ghetto, however, by virtue of drawing upon his ethico-religious resources, he was not as prone to experience a high degree of "analytic, emotional, and moral impotence" in the face of evil, suffering and death, that is, he could tolerate the conditions better than the more secular inmates, who were mostly assimilated, middle-class Jews from, for example, Czechoslovakia, Germany, Austria and Holland.

Baeck had, in his view, a God-inspired sacred moral code (e.g., the Talmud) to give direction to his actions when he was faced "with intractable ethical paradox, the disquieting sense that one's moral insight is inadequate to one's moral experience" (Geertz, 1973, p. 106).

Though devout Jews like Baeck had their doubts, uncertainties, questions, and made protests to their God for their suffering and the evil they were facing, they did have faith that, while elusive, there must be a moral, intellectual, and emotional explanation for their encounter with evil. The certainty that there was a principle or explanation that could, and maybe would, in this world or the next, eventually make their suffering intelligible and meaningful, meant that they could sustain important aspects of the moral structures of their world. The believing inmates thus maintained a relative sense of agency, efficacy, and control over their situation.

It should be noted, however, that the above findings are not in harmony with Levinas's novel thinking about suffering. For Levinas, qua Holocaust survivor,[16] we reside in an era "of gratuitous human suffering, in which evil appears in its diabolical horror," in an era that reflects the "end of theodicy" in both its theological and secular expressions, such as in atheistic progressivism. That is, theodicy is a seductive "temptation," an effort "in making God innocent, or in saving morality in the name of faith, or in making suffering bearable" (Levinas, 1998, pp. 96–97). For Levinas, intellectual integrity demands that any attempts to justify or reconcile ourselves to useless, meaningless, unendurable suffering, as in the Holocaust, Hiroshima or the Gulag, is futile and disingenuous. Theodicy is over, Levinas boldly declares (Bernstein, 2002, p. 255). He is of course right in a certain sense. There are no grand theodicies that account for the Holocaust and similar horrors that are generally regarded as adequate and satisfying, that settle the problem of evil and undeserved suffering.[17] However, Levinas is incorrect when it comes to the real-life, hellish world of the Kingdom of Night. As I have reported, eye witness accounts and compelling testimonials of concentration camp inmates and survivors, like Bettelheim, Améry, Levi, Wiesel, Frankel, and Pawelczyńska, at least on the level of the individual trying to sustain himself as a person, to preserve his autonomy, integration and humanity, challenge Levinas's sweeping conclusion that theodicy and other such self-sustaining, transcendent notions, are over. Berkovits (1979) provides many examples of the religious Jew's use of theodicy to help concentration camp and ghetto inmates maintain their autonomy, integration and humanity.

From 1945–1956, despite his experience in Theresienstadt, Baeck "did not feel that the Holocaust had changed anything he believed, and he did not see it requiring him to rewrite what he had said so powerfully in an earlier, happy time" (Borowitz, 1983, p. 63). For Baeck, evil, even the radical evil of the Nazis, was the consequence of free human choice, and God dignified us as humans by not interfering with the freedom to determine what we do. For God to remove that freedom due to our abusing it would itself be evil, a dangerous betrayal of human responsibility (Borowitz, 1983, p. 63). While the Nazis were worse than any other tyrannical regime aiming to destroy the Jewish people, it did not fundamentally alter the problem of evil, that is, theodicy (Borowitz, 1983, p. 63). As Feller noted, "Suffering in the *Essence* was connected for Baeck to the Jewish task in the world. Both were consequences of Jews striving toward the One God and a more ethical world. Jewish suffering was also a measurement for how this ideal still was" (Feller, 2024, p. 93). One of Baeck's main beliefs was that "the Jewish minority is the yardstick of morality and a bearer of ethics" (Feller, 2024, p. 181).

Conclusion

Baeck appears to have been lodged in a religious, symbolic world, one that sociologist Peter Berger famously called a "sacred canopy." To some extent, relatively speaking, Baeck was consciously and unconsciously able to effectively assimilate the emotionally dissonant experiences of his ordeal of suffering in Theresienstadt, "into a comprehensive explanation of reality and human destiny" (Berger & Berger, 1972, p. 352). Put differently, Baeck had a "vision of reality," a system of meaning and metaphor that helped him endure, the illness, death and despair he was mired in (Schafer, 1976, p. 22). For Baeck, traditional Judaism, albeit with a liberal texturing, was largely his symbolic world that operated as a sacred canopy, at least to some extent. Such a symbolic world gave Baeck the will and ability to express his goodness.

As Berger further notes, "religion shows most clearly its function of providing ultimate meaning for human life in its ability to integrate the painful and terrifying experiences of life, and even death itself," into a theodicy, an explanation for evil and prosperity (Berger & Berger, 1972, p. 352). In *The Sacred Canopy* (1967), Berger defines religion as "the establishment, through human activity, of an all-embracing sacred order, that is, of a sacred cosmos that will be capable of maintaining itself in the ever-present face of chaos" (Berger, 1967, p. 51). Indeed, as I have suggested, life in Theresienstadt was chaotic, for the most part, it shattered any sense of safety, meaning and narrative.

By conceptualizing religion in this manner and situating it in reference to everyday life, helps to shed light on some of its important functions for Baeck, as a ghetto inmate. As Wuthnow (2024, n.p.) summarizes the matter, religious teachings typically serve to shelter the individual from chaos, from a reality that seems to make no or little sense, by providing explanations for suffering, death, tragedy and injustice. As I have said earlier, Baeck believed that the radical evil of the Nazis was the consequence of free human choice, it was not God-made, and thus the lynchpin of his belief and value system, belief in an immanent and transcendent God, remained relatively intact. As a result of the aforementioned, Baeck was better able integrate his biography by providing an overarching frame of reference that applied to all of life, that located him in space and time, that specified an ultimate purpose for his individual life, and thus allowed daily activities to be organized around the fulfillment of this purpose (Wuthnow, 2024).

In addition to religious teachings, "religious rituals provide[d] mechanisms for containing the potentially disruptive experiences of mourning on the one hand, or, of transcendent joy on the other" (Wuthnow, 2024). Funerals, Bar Mitzvahs, weddings, and other religiously orchestrated rites of passages maintained the stability of Baeck's everyday life by providing occasions on which the non-ordinary could be experienced. Put differently, Baeck's Judaism was a reality that drew from cultural materials, that were filtered through the symbolically constructed reality of his personal experience. In addition, this reality was sustained through the social interaction of his flock and other individuals. While Berger gives special attention to religious symbolism, he also realizes the importance of synagogues and worship services, for the perpetuation of Judaism, modified as it was, in Theresienstadt. Thus, we can say, that it was to some extent via his understanding and practice of traditional Judaism with a liberal texturing, his symbolic resources, that Baeck was better able to maintain the rudiments of his autonomy, integration and humanity, this being the foundation of his goodness.

Berger, and Wuthnow in his analysis of the *Sacred Canopy*, emphasize the relationship between religious symbolism and social interaction by suggesting a dialectic interplay between the two. This aspect of *The Sacred Canopy* has bearing on Baeck's way of being-in-the-world in Theresienstadt.

Assuming that man is a meaning-seeking (and affect-integrating and action-guiding) entity, one that seeks out an all-embracing, overarching meaning, Berger alleges the emergence of a religious symbol system like Judaism, in part, as a consequence of the individual interacting with others in similar circumstances, that is, Baeck's fellow inmates in Theresienstadt, helped these inmates maintain a modicum of their autonomy, integration and humanity. Berger calls this "externalization." That is, "the subjective moods and motivations of these individuals become an external reality in the form of concrete symbols that can be discussed and acted upon" (Wuthnow, 2024, n.p.). Berger defines externalization as "the ongoing outpouring of human being into the world, both in the physical and mental activity of men" (Berger, 1967, p. 4).

The second phase of the development of this emergent symbol system becomes "objectified." In other words, through additional interaction it stops being the creation of any single individual but rather becomes something "out there" that may even be codified in formal creeds and sacred writings. Berger defines objectification as "the attainment by the products of this activity (again both physical and mental) of a reality that confronts its original producers as a facticity [a condition of fact] external to and other than themselves" (Berger, 1967, p. 4).

For Baeck and other devout Jews, God was an external other that had objective meaning and purpose, and to which one was obligated to obey. As Wuthnow further notes, "no longer is it something that someone 'made up' or has control over; rather, it is a feature of the outside world – a set of creeds, rituals, and institutions – that confronts the individual with an authority of its own" (Wuthnow, 2024, n.p.). In other words, Baeck and other devout Jews had faith in what they perceived as an objective moral order.

Finally, "this reality is 'internalized,' becoming once again part of the individual's subjective identity" (Wuthnow, 2024, n.p.). "Internalization," says Berger, "is the reappropriation by men of this same reality, transforming it once again from structures of the objective world into structures of the subjective consciousness" (Berger, 1967, p. 4). For Baeck, such an outlook played out in his view of reality and his way of dealing with it. Referring to religious and political inmates in Auschwitz:

> He [the believer, Baeck] is both estranged from reality and closer to it than the unbelieving comrade. Further from reality because in his Finalistic attitude he ignores the given contents of material phenomenon and fixes his sight on a nearer or more distant future; but he is also closer to reality because for just this reason he does not allow himself to be overwhelmed by the conditions around him and thus can strongly influence them. For the unbelieving person, reality, under adverse circumstances, is a force to which he submits; under favorable ones it is material for analysis. For the believer, reality is clay that molds, a problem that he solves.
>
> *(Améry, 1980, p. 14)*

As Geertz notes, the religious perspective questions everyday reality in terms of a "wider, non-hypothetical" truth. "Detachment" and "analysis," the watchwords of the psychoanalytic intellectual (at least of the Freudian variety), are replaced by "commitment" and "encounter," if you will, subjectivity. It is "the imbuing of a certain specific complex of symbols—of the metaphysic they formulate and the style of life they recommend—with a persuasive authority which, from an analytic point of view, is the essence of religious action" (Geertz, 1973, p. 112). In the camps, including to some degree in Theresienstadt, this meant that religious inmates had the symbolic capacity to transform their reality, at least to some extent, and episodically, into something other than the dehumanizing reality. Through their faith, including the rituals that they participated in, frequently in a communal context, they had the ability to move beyond the realties of everyday life to more transcendent realities that, says Geertz, corrected and completed the painful realities of the ghetto.

Berkovits (1979) describes how religious Jews in the death camps and ghettos "imposed another rhythm on the raw reality to which they were subjected and thus drew out its dehumanizing poison." "The authentic Jewish lifestyle," says Berkovits—like the various places in the Holocaust kingdom where *sukkot* were built secretly, or the hiding places for *tefillin*, for a Hanukkah menorah, for a shofar to blow on Rosh Hashanah—all points to a superimposition of "a space-structure of meaningfulness on the camp geography of humiliation and degradation . . . an autonomous restructuring of camp reality" (pp. 64, 65).

In light of the aforementioned, how then did Baeck maintain the rudiments of his autonomy, integration and humanity in Theresienstadt? He was willing and able to use the spiritual resources emanating from his symbolic universe, his version of traditional Judaism, as a sacred canopy. Through his personal observance, through what he described as "prayer and study," as well as giving lectures to his fellow inmates, facilitating discussion groups, especially on Jewish themes, his practice of Judaism amidst extremity, such as officiating over Passover and Purim holidays, as well as Bar Mitzvahs, weddings and the like, through his theodicy that blamed his incarceration on man's choice of evil, not God-made, he was able to maintain the coordinates of his pre-incarceration narrative of self-identity (e.g., his self-esteem, self-continuity and self-cohesion). Baeck, in other words, viewed himself as witness. It was Baeck's use of his passionately felt, transcendent-pointing moral beliefs and values that appears to have made the difference between maintaining a degree of his autonomy, integration and humanity in Theresienstadt. Such psychic accomplishments were a fertile breeding ground for Baeck's expression of goodness.

These findings for the most part, agree with Bettelheim, Levi, Améry, Frankl, Wiesel, Pawelczyńska, and Todorov among others, even though the aforementioned were concentration and death camps survivors. As Baeck succinctly put it, without his religious faith to nourish and stabilize him, he would not have been willing and able to stay "spiritually healthy" (Feller, 2024, p. 178), a vital resource in the struggle to remain human.

Notes

1 On the other hand, not only were there non-Jews in Theresienstadt, but most Jews were assimilated, thus, one could argue that Verdi's *Requiem* was part of European culture (Meyer, 2024).

2 The inspection took place on June 23, 1944. This visit is noteworthy for the controversial report that characterized the camp conditions as better than they in fact were, which is regarded as a crucial failure of the International Committee of the Red Cross during the Holocaust (see https://www.icrc.org/en/document/icrc-wwii-holocaust, accessed November 23, 2024).

3 See Marcus (1999) for an extensive discussion of "choiceless choice." Hájková (2020) also has a critical "take" on this notion.

4 About 87,000 inmates were deported from Theresienstadt, only about 4,000 survived; 84 percent of the elderly died in the ghetto; 34,000 inmates died in Theresienstadt (Hájková, 2020). Indeed, Theresienstadt was a death world.

5 Adler developed an inmate typology that involved fourteen types of inmates: The broken, the fearful, the numb, the heedless, pessimists, realists, optimists, illusionists, active people, brutal people, opportunists, strong-willed people, helpers, and kindhearted people (p. 589). Obviously, there was overlap in these ideal types, for example, from what I can discern, Baeck was kindhearted, optimistic, realistic, active, strong-willed and a helper.

6 Hájková (2020) noted that in Theresienstadt intimacy and attachment were important coping mechanisms for the typical inmate.

7 It is important to appreciate the context of Wiesel's remarks for, as far as I can tell, they have a somewhat rhetorical quality. Wiesel made his comments as part of his improvised reply to a controversial lecture given by Richard Rubenstein (a death of God theologian) to the question of "What can be told, what can be written, where must silence be kept, what can be witnessed only by living?" (the quote is cited by the editors, p. 269).

8 *Reichsvertretung der Deutschen Juden* [The Reich Representation of German Jews] was a Jewish umbrella organization started in 1933.

9 Said Frankl, "If the man in the concentration camp did not struggle against this [the loss of human values] in a last effort to save his self-respect, he lost the feeling of being an individual, a being with a mind, with inner freedom and personal value; he thought of himself as only a part of an enormous mass of people" (Berkovits, 1979, p. 57).

10 Detailing this splitting process is beyond the scope of this book, see Marcus (1999) for an extended critical discussion of splitting viewed psychoanalytically. Hájková (2020) mentions that inmates were capable of compartmentalizing their danger in Theresienstadt.

11 In Jewish tradition, martyrdom is commanded in opposition to three sins: murder, adultery (incest) and idolatry.

12 As Person et al. (2005) notes, a selfobject is "the individual's experience of another person as functioning as part of the self or as necessary to fulfill a need of the self" (p. 559).

13 Adler (2022 [1955]) notes that "religious life played a relatively minor role, and it also remained on the sidelines officially" (p. 539). This being said, Adler describes what religious life there was in Theresienstadt in a manner that resonates with Baker's description as well as Baeck's other biographer (Meyer, 2021).

14 Baeck conducted a funeral for the daughter of Theodore Herzl, the founder of political Zionism (Meyer, 2021). Also, it is worth noting, Martha Cohen, Hermann Cohen's wife died in Theresienstadt (Hermann Cohen died in 1918).

15 As Baker (1978) noted, "By the fall of 1942 Theresienstadt built to hold perhaps 10,000 people at most, housed more than 60,000 Jews" (p. 283).

16 Levinas was incarcerated in a prisoner of war camp, following surrender of his military unit.

17 For example, before he died in 2020, the Chief Rabbi of the UK, Jonathan Sacks wrote that "When bad things happen to us it is because we have been guilty of doing bad things to ourselves. . . . If bad things have happened let us blame no one but ourselves, and let us labour to make things better" (Sacks, 2024b, pp. 1–2). Sacks appears to simplistically blame the victim for his undeserved suffering.

4

RELIGIOUS CONSCIOUSNESS AND THEOLOGICAL REFLECTIONS

Baeck developed what has been called a "*theologia viatorum*," the theology of travelers (Friedlander, 1968, p. 155), calling to mind Gabriel Marcel's famous term *homo viator*, itinerant traveler, both terms suggesting that life is viewed as a challenging journey, stressing mortality saliency, the fact that living is a transient, if not fleeting experience. As the great philosopher/theologian Paul Tillich noted, mortality saliency makes existence a matter of "ultimate concern," that is, the state of being-in-the-world we all tend to experience throughout the life-cycle that defines us and our beliefs and values. Religious consciousness is a mindfulness of God and of others in God. It is not simply a feeling, though it may be complimented by feelings. It is not simply a thought, though it is conscious and may be thought about and reflected on. Baeck was steeped in a religious consciousness, traditional Judaism (with a liberal bent), in his overall outlook and behavior. One of the main characteristic aspects of Judaism's understanding of the relation between the person and God, said Baeck, was the "consciousness of being created" (Pasachoff, 1992, p. 149). That is, "To be both created and yet creator is the heart of Jewish religious consciousness" (Pasachoff, 1992, p. 159). This outlook potentiated the feeling of reverence and humility, psychic accomplishments that helped Baeck actualize goodness.

As Meyer (1999) has noted, central to Baeck's philosophy of adversity is the notion of divine commandment, especially when it is paired with mystery.[1] By commandment, Baeck is referencing the fact that in his view, "commandment and duty" are "the paramount factor of religion . . . to make the ethical the center of religion is the special characteristic of monotheism" (Baeck, 1948, pp. 70, 95). Ethical monotheism was the great Jewish contribution to religious thought. On commandment:

> If love tells man what he is because of God, then justice tells him what he ought to be before God. And only the two together are a full revelation of the

DOI: 10.4324/9781003534327-4

> One God; only the two together disclose the full meaning of human existence. Through their unity is revealed the deeper content of the unity of God. It is a special characteristic of this unity that the hidden and unfathomable elements of our life tell us of the love of God while the clear and definite elements tell us of God's commanding justice. It is man as an individual who experiences all this; the commandment speaks to the personality. He hears the question put to him by God, 'Where art thou?'
>
> *(Baeck, 1948, p. 122)*

The aforementioned calls to mind Levinas's notion of Abraham being summoned by God to serve Him, to sacrifice his son Isaac, and his response, "*Hineni*," here I am. Likewise, Moses says *Hineni* when standing before the burning bush.

Baeck further notes that it is via moral action that man becomes authentically humble. In this way, says Baeck, "does faith become a commandment; believe thou ever more profoundly in God by ever doing more good!" (1948, p. 134). Baeck is here making the moral deed the highest Jewish value, "an infinite ethical demand," and this assumes and ethical outlook that is first and foremost lodged in a profound belief in God: "In its eyes morality has its foundation and guarantee in God" (1948, pp. 172, 148). As Meyer noted, "Baeck reduced the divine imperative to one. Mostly he did not specify its contents, leaving it simply as 'Thou shalt . . .!' It thus became a generalized unconditional commandment to do good as the human being understands it" (Meyer, 1999, p. 109).

I have earlier suggested that the "full implications" of Baeck's theology "emerge only when the work is placed into the life of the author" (Friedlander, 2024, n.p.) That is, Baeck the man and his scholarly work are unusually blended and they are best amalgamated in order to get a sense of the person (he had a consistency of thought, teaching and action (Brann, 1963)). Indeed, as Sartre said somewhere, every book is an attempt by the author to improve his biography. For example, Friedlander noted about Baeck's magnum opus which I have liberally quoted from, "The *Essence of Judaism* has an autobiographical aspect" (Friedlander, 1968, p. 63) as did his landmark essay "Mystery and Commandment" (Friedlander, 1968, p. 170). In other words, Baeck's aforementioned assertions about commandment and the like, are lodged in a conception of the conscience and the human condition in which obligation and duty are paramount in serving God. Psychoanalytically, one could simply say, that Baeck personifies a high functioning super-ego (roughly, the conscience), one that does not shirk responsibility towards the other, and is not prone to excessive guilt or shame for unintentional acts of omission or commission. Indeed, being steeped in such an outlook may have in part, motivated Baeck to graciously offer succor to his flock both inside and outside of Theresienstadt. Put differently, using Adler's typological categories, Baeck was inclined to be kindhearted and a helper, as a function of his religious outlook and his correlated personality dynamics.

Being a religious man, Baeck believed that sanctification itself lay in the moral realm (Meyer, 1999). He thus organizationally applied the categories of sacred and profane in a similar manner as he did those ethical categories of good and evil (1999, p. 109). What is important to remember is that for Baeck, ethics is lodged in the mysterious grounding in God (Borowitz, 1983) and the main thrust of holiness is a way of being-in-the-world that is other-directed, other-regarding and other-serving, especially other-serving, for example, as demonstrated in Baeck's compassionate and supportive outlook and behavior inside and outside of Theresienstadt. As Baeck notes,

> If a man is to be holy as God is holy, or as another Biblical expression has it, if he is 'to walk in all His ways, and to love Him,' [Deut. 10:12] if his life is to be thus measured by the supreme, divine standard, his task is never finished.
>
> *(Baeck, 1958, p. 45)*

For Baeck, while Jewish ritual was sacred in terms of its impact on the believer, the ritual *mitzvoth* (commandments) themselves did not have any intrinsic religious significance except in the secondary sense (Meyer, 1999). As Meyer notes,

> In line with the Reform movement, with which he identified as a Liberal rabbi, he believed in ritual laws (which he personally observed), by focusing mind and emotion on the moral role of the human being, were a means to the end of sanctification, but they did not possess intrinsic moral value.
>
> *(Meyer, 1999, p. 109).*

Thus, for Baeck, the commanding God spoke directly to man, to the inviolate indestructible core of his conscience, that demanded a holy response, one that was ethical, that is, as Levinas says, being-for-the-other, often before oneself (Baeck, 1958). Such a way of being was as Hindu Indians say, part doctor and part priest (or rabbi!). By behaving in a holy manner, at least some of the time, Baeck was able to maintain the rudiments of his pre-imprisonment sense of self.

Prophetic Judaism

Baeck's beliefs and values were anchored in prophetic Judaism (Baeck, 1958). The prophets memorialized their prophecies in writing, as they were chosen by God during a period of social and political unrest and crisis, if not disaster, in the community. Their role was to warn, castigate the morals and ethics of their day, and advise and comfort the people of Israel. As Baeck noted, "it was they who gave Judaism its spiritual direction—and while it is true that Judaism deviated at times, in the end it returned to the course they had chartered." Most importantly, the prophets gave the Jewish people "that spiritual kernel of Judaism, which persisted through the sifting of time. In their thoughts, Judaism found its goal and its truth; they created its history" (Baeck, 1948, p. 31). As Baeck explains, all the features of Judaism "show it to be a prophetic creation stressing not the abstract conceptions but rather man, his life and conscience," that is, "the religion of the prophets strives to enter the personality of every man" (Baeck, 1948, pp. 41, 46). In other words, through relating to others with love and justice, by embracing a political morality that demanded always treating others as ends in themselves (Katz, 2014), the prophetic task is assigned to everyone (Baeck, 1958). The religious life is thus quite literally "a process of spiritual self-awareness, self-assertion and self-creation" (Lichtenstein, 1963, p. 288).

Baeck describes some of the qualities of mind and heart that the prophet personifies, that resonates with himself and he believes, with Jewish identity in general. To the prophets, religion was "the meaning, the innermost core of their existence and not something which has been acquired or learned" (Baeck, 1948, p. 34). Put differently, "man lives neither for nor on his emotional moods," rather, "in the pious deed is the sustaining foundation of the confession of faith" (Baeck, 1948, pp. 55, 56). "Faith is performing His will," Baeck quoted from one of the books of wisdom (Baeck, 1964, p. 25).

First, the most important aspect of the prophetic vision was its intuitive and practical character. The thoughts of the prophets emanate from the heart not merely from the head, they have as a motivator an "ethical urge – they are overwhelmed by an irresistible truth" (Baeck, 1964 [1955], p. 32).

Says Baeck, "They speak because they must speak, and it is this inner compulsion which so convinces us that we hear in them the voice of conscience. What they say was given to them by God" (Baeck, 1964 [1955]). Such a "'daimonic power,'" says Baeck, this inner conviction of revelation, is the spiritual particularity of the workings of the prophet. These "geniuses of religion" were not only teachers who in times of moral ambiguity and uncertainty told to the Israelites what was right or wrong, in addition, they spoke with the compelling voice of God, "full of power by the spirit of the Lord" (Baeck, 1964 [1955]).

Second, the prophets had the will and ability to exercise human choice: "They reveal themselves to God while God reveals himself to them; God orders them to speak and they speak and strive with him" (Baeck, 1964 [1955], p. 33). Thus, there is a double structure to their way of being-in-the-world that assumes a unity of feeling, thinking and acting.

Third, the prophets do not view their experience of God, their knowledge of Him as the consequence of mere intellectual speculation. To the prophets, religion is the meaning, the innermost aspect of their way of being-in-the-world and not something external which has been acquired or learned. In other words, for the prophets, it was not a matter of providing a logical exposition of God's existence, rather, the contradictions and incomprehensibilities were painfully revealed by these men and women of God (Baeck, 1964, p. 33).

Fourth, the "free conviction of inner connectedness with God constitutes the unique ethical basis of the words of the prophets" which has always been the hallmark of Judaism. That is, the free will, responsibility and conscience, as the foundation of their spiritual experience, are assumed as much as is the sanctity of God (Baeck, 1964 [1955], p. 34).

Fifth, prophets use the expression "to know God" as their typical way of reflecting on their experience. Whatever cognitions the prophets have refer not to something beyond ordinary experience, but rather, it is something that remains within the domain of ethical considerations, of ethical monotheism. "To know God and to do right have thus become synonymous in prophetic speech" (Baeck, 1964 [1955], p. 37). What is key here is that for the prophets what matters most is the right deed, and with this deed goes the revealed knowledge. Right living potentiates right thinking. *Na'aseh V'nishma,* we'll do (obey), and then we'll listen (learn). As Baeck says, "There is no piety but that which proves itself in the conduct of life, and there is no valid conduct of life but that in which religion is realized" (Baeck, 1964 [1955], p. 37).

Sixth, the prophets are dedicated to ethicality lodged in the here-and-now, they are not interested in life after death, in the world to come, let alone logical proofs of God's existence. Rather, their emphasis is on the commandment to man, "thus shalt thou live," which overrides any talk of an afterlife and the like (Baeck, 1964 [1955], p. 37). As Baeck notes, "the prophetic word is a living and personal confession of faith which cannot be circumscribed by rigid boundaries; it possesses a breadth and a freedom carrying within itself the possibilities of revival and development" (Baeck, 1964 [1955], p. 43). The prophets were thus anti-systematic, fearing that their passionate message would not be properly embraced. As Meyer (2021) points out, "the prophets embody the essence of Judaism, which Baeck defines as the unmitigated moral imperative" (p. 24). Put differently, "for Baeck, the essence of Judaism is the divine command to redeem mankind from evil through justice and love" (Brann, 1963, p. 151). This is another way of referencing the enactment of goodness.

In summary, we can say that while Baeck was not a prophet, he often behaved in a manner that calls to mind the prophetic. A man touched, if not transformed by the Divine (Friedlander, 1968). The foundation of the prophet's strength was their experience of a loving and just God, and their closeness to Him was expressed through their unselfishness and skillful discernment. They saw things through their own eyes according to their circumstances. They spoke in the language and understanding of the people of their day. Individual prophets were raised up at particular times to fill a special need and Baeck appeared to rise to the occasion vis-à-vis the needs of the Jewish community both inside and outside of Theresienstadt. The prophet was an impressive instance of establishing truthfulness, selflessness, ethics, reliability, loyalty and passion, in Baeck's case this was during his tenure as leader of the German-Jewish community inside and outside of Theresienstadt. Based on extensive interviews, Hájková summarizes Baeck's way of comporting himself in Theresienstadt:

> Leo Baeck is the best example of someone being able to establish unofficial power within the ghetto. The many stories told about Leo Baeck in Theresienstadt depicts a moral force in the face of corruption and folly, a man who led the prisoners during difficult times. . . . Baeck invested considerable energy

> in getting along with other inmates, almost everyone remembered him in an extremely positive light. Repeatedly he was described as wise and friendly, but aloof. It is remarkable that Baeck got along with people who had opposing opinions and were very critical of each other. Almost everyone admired him. . . . Indeed, all his life Baeck was described as a tolerant and pluralist personality.
>
> *(Hájková, 2020, pp. 50, 52)*[2]

What is particularly interesting to note is that Baeck's identification with the prophetic tradition cast him in the role of Jewish witness. While in Theresienstadt, Baeck "saw himself as a witness to the existence of another world beyond this fatal 'ghetto'" (Adler, 2022 [1955], p. 215). In other words, Baeck may have seen himself as a deliverer of a message from God, a bearer of the divine word with a degree of authority in the ghetto context (as he did have unofficial power in Theresienstadt).[3] Baeck had consistently asserted "his belief in the value of Judaism as an ethical force in the world" (Feller, 2024, p. 16). The important point to be mindful of is that for Baeck, being lodged in a prophetic Judaism gave to his life both "meaning and purpose" which were the resources by which his life was authentically realized inside and outside of Theresienstadt (Baeck, 1948, p. 142). Baeck said that:

> The possibility of conflict between faith and life is removed by the prophets' insistence that religion has to be realized through life [through goodness], while faith and knowledge are reconciled by the insistence that religion is not to be proved by means of knowledge.
>
> *(Brann, 1963, p. 153)*

Jewish History and Jewish People

Baeck understood Jewish history to be one "of affirming or rejecting God's covenant with Israel" (Meyer, 1999, p. 110). As previously stated, Baeck has been described as a man affected by the Divine. When Baeck, qua religious Jew, recognized the divine imperative, the outcome is a tension that can be faced or ignored. In that tension, says Meyer, "theology and history meet."

> This problem, through which Judaism in all its particularity and on account of its particularity has become universal, this specifically Jewish world-historical problem, is that of the incursion of the infinite, eternal, one, and unlimited into the finite, temporal, manifold, and of the spiritual, moral tension of the human fiber that it creates. All the ideas and hopes that Judaism has produced within its own realm and beyond it originate here.
>
> *(Meyer, 1999, pp. 110–111)*

Exactly in what manner this aforementioned tension was dealt with made all the difference in Baeck's life. Rejection of the tension would be equivalent to the rejection of the revealing God, however, acceptance is the decision to do God's work on earth, an important aspect of Baeck's motivation to behave in such a kindhearted and helpful manner (i.e., goodness) throughout his ordeal of suffering (Meyer, 1999, p. 111). In Baeck's view, one of the important aspects of Jewish history was this assuming of a comportment that led to specific qualities of character. Not only did such an outlook include humility given the magnitude and depth of the task to be completed, but it also required the capacity to be oppositional and defiant, a quality of the Jew in history: "The Jewish task was to be nonconformist" (Meyer, 1999, p. 111), a quality of mind and heart that the Jew at his best, has assumed throughout its long history (think of Marx, Freud, and Einstein, for example). It was precisely this context, "eternal nonconformity" as Baeck called it (Meyer 2021, p. 123) that Baeck was lodged in while in Nazi Germany and later, in Theresienstadt. This required imagination, "the vision that ever again and in spite of everything makes him see a future;" and patience, "this power of resilience that did not let the will to live give way" (Baker, 1978 p. 295).

Thus, in terms of Baeck's understanding of the Jewish people and Jewish history, we can say that he had a specific combination of particularism and universalism, the former especially when we consider the notion of the "chosen people." As Borowitz notes, "in Baeck's system, religious consciousness allows us to conceive God via our sense of the mysterious depth to human createdness":

> They [the Jewish people] felt themselves uniquely pledged to God and historically identified with the idea of ethical monotheism. They thus became a people with a mission. They survived as a people not only for their own sake, but so that humankind might come to know and serve the one God. In this knowledge they found the strength to endure their suffering over the millennia.
>
> *(Borowitz, 1983, p. 67)*

For Baeck, says Borowitz, the Jews were "chosen" because they chose to dedicate themselves to God (not because they had any inherent superiority). They were faced, as all people are, with God's command to be the best of being human, "but also alone made that behest the foundation of their ethnic life." This in turn "became their deepest consciousness of themselves," thus they narrated themselves as God's chosen people (Borowitz, 1983, p. 67).

With regards the Jewish role in history, Baeck believed that contemporary Jews should engage in a campaign of proselytization. In his view of history, when Jews are free agents, they often proselytized. Therefore, says Borowitz, Jews today, "in all dignity and faithfulness to their belief, they should do it again" (Borowitz, 1983, p. 69). Baeck maintained that ethical monotheism is associated with the Jewish people and "stubborn endurance is a Jewish ethical imperative; for a Jew, to exist is a commandment" (Borowitz, 1983, p. 69).[4] Said Baeck, "To rouse the conscience of humanity could be our best title-deed," a manifestation of goodness (Meyer, 2021, p. 173). That is, as Meyer notes, the goal was "to set the world right under the sovereignty of God" (Meyer, 2021, p. 173).

Whatever one thinks of Baeck's interpretation of the chosen people and proselytizing notions, what appears to be the case is that he very much believed what he wrote. As a result of this, Baeck was part of a long chain of Jewish continuity that in part, gave him the will and ability to press on despite the hardships he endured.

Romantic versus Classical Religion

In *The Essence of Judaism*, Baeck contrasts Judaism, the religion of ethical optimism that is world-affirming with Buddhism a religion that despite its ethical outlook of a sort, is fundamentally pessimistic and world-rejecting (Borowitz, 1983).

> Judaism leads to the desire to work for the kingdom of God in which all men may unite, while Buddhism leads to the desire to sink into the One [mystical immersion in the absolute], into nothingness, there to find deliverance and salvation for the ego.[5] Judaism calls for ascent, development, the long march toward the future, while Buddhism preaches return, cessation, futureless existence in silence. Judaism seeks to reconcile the world with God while Buddhism tries to escape from the world. Judaism demands creation, new men and a new world; Buddhism seeks 'extinction,' departure from humanity and from the world.
>
> *(Baeck, 1948, p. 60)*

Thus, concludes Baeck, "Judaism is a religion of altruism," as it proclaims man to be striving toward moral perfection, his way to God, by seeking his fellow humans, and who serves God by loving and being just to them. In contrast, Baeck alleges, Buddhism is "the religion of egotism," since it identifies perfection to the man who retreats from mankind in order to discover the only true approach to himself. Judaism then, is "the religion of revelation," a "classical manifestation of religion" (Baeck, 1948, p. 61). By revelation Baeck means, Israel's aptitude to live within the creative tension between mystery and commandment, in a religion of ethical mindfulness that has remained conscious of its ultimate foundation in the Infinite (Friedlander, 1968). For Baeck then, "Theology is man's search for the Divine within the realm of man, the content of life in which man discovers the foundation of life" (Friedlander, 1968, p. 158). That is, according to Baeck, "the fundamental concern of theology was man's ethical response to the Divine revelation" (Friedlander, 1968, p. 154), the cultivation of goodness.

Despite Baeck's somewhat oversimplified rendering of Buddhist thought, he seems to be saying that Jewish particularity has "existential validity," since it is the Jewish community that carries ethical monotheism through history. In Baeck's view, Christianity has some common ethical ground with Judaism however, Baeck strongly believes that "Christian self-consciousness" is markedly different compared to its Jewish counterpart (Borowitz, 1983, p. 68).

In a famous essay entitled 'Romantic Religion' (Baeck, 1981a [1958]), Baeck contrasts Judaism with Paul and Luther, among others. While I will not give here a detailed analysis of the lengthy, and now somewhat dated, essay, what is important from our perspective, is that Baeck uses a typological method to characterize two types of religious experience: Classical and Romantic (Borowitz, 1983).

Classical religion of which Judaism is the paradigm, Baeck claims, "is positive, activist, outgoing, social, ethical, deed-oriented, rational [and] masculine" (Baeck, 1981a [1958]), p. 68). In contrast, Romantic religion of which Christianity is the paradigm, is passive in its confrontation with reality, individualistic, self-centered, inward-focused, concerned with faith and its content, confirming itself in feeling-states, stressing grace, and has a feminine feel to it (Baeck, 1981a [1958]). As Baeck summarizes the matter with regards to the subject of redemption:

> The ideal of the romantic looks altogether different. For him the highest aim is the achieved redemption, the quintessence of being beyond the Law, or pure abandonment of self. This is the end of romantic religion. All romantic faith is such redemption. It is fulfillment of the longing for passivity, of the desire to be rid of the commanding will, of the craving to be seized and to experience absolute dependence.
>
> *(Baeck, 1981a [1958], p. 176)*

Moreover, says Baeck,

> Redemption has nothing whatever to do with the exertions and tasks of the inner life, with the struggles and responses of conscience, with the wrestling and ultimate peace of the soul, with ethical striving and ethical freedom. Redemption in this sense does not signify an unfolding of human nature, and arduous ascent, any triumph over sin—altogether nothing can be commanded—it is a supernatural process, determined by the chance of fate and accomplished by a miracle.
>
> *(Baeck, 1981a [1958])*

In 'Romantic Religion,' Baeck cast his net very widely, covering the range of Christian history, Catholic and Protestant, to demonstrate its non-rational, ethics-subordinating aspects (Borowitz, 1983). As Borowitz further notes, "Since these are fundamental to Christianity as a religion, in principle it cannot hope to become a more activist, ethical faith by accepting liberal ideas." Judaism, however, has always been "of world-transforming ethical monotheism so its modernization is only the fulfillment of its classic stance" (Borowitz, 1983, p. 68).

As Meyer (2021) points out, Baeck's agenda was to critically evaluate Paul and Luther, on the way to differentiating Judaism from Christianity, alleging that the former is superior to the latter, the opposite to what Harnack, the Lutheran theologian, alleged. This was not a mere scholarly undertaking, but in addition Baeck wanted "to justify the continued existence of a separate and, he believed morally superior Jewish faith" (p. 19). 'Romantic Religion' was written in 1922 (the version I am citing was written after that date), and notwithstanding the oversimplification and selective readings of Christianity, Baeck needed to protect Judaism from attack by Harnack, while at the same time affirming Judaism's superiority. In this way, he and his community were able to sustain itself amidst the gathering storm that culminated in Nazi Germany. As Borowitz notes in his criticisms of Baeck's essay, "Baeck's argument for Jewish uniqueness says more about Baeck's love for his tradition than it does about reality" (Borowitz, 1983, p. 69).

Thus, as Baker (1978) points out, the significance of the essay is threefold. First, on the manifest level, it is a polemic against Christianity, it was a defense of Judaism against over 2000 years of antisemitic attacks. Second, the essay was written when there were early indications of the eventual failure of the Weimar Republic; Baeck was pleading to all believers, regardless of their religion, to recognize and affirm the fact that above all else, religion requires morality. As Baker further notes, "The purpose of religion is not the individual's personal salvation, but, rather, the individual's impact on the salvation of others" (Baker, 1978, p. 130). Third, this essay was a call to fellow Jews to rid themselves of their apologetic outlook: "Do not be embarrassed by your religion, particularly when it is compared to Christianity. Judaism is the superior of the two, and the central fact of Christianity—the presence of Jesus—is actually a Jewish presence" (Baker, 1978, p. 130).

That is, Baeck fought against antisemitism by emphasizing the Jewishness of Christianity (Feller, 2024). His overarching goal was that the two great religions would understand each other better and thereby more amicably co-exist.

A Brief Word on the Psychic Function of Baeck's Scholarly Writing

Baeck wrote the important and extensive volume, *This People Israel: The Meaning of Jewish Existence*, while in Theresienstadt on random scraps of paper. He completed the book after the war. In my view, this book, his lecturing, especially on Jewish topics, in the ghetto, and probably many of his scholarly writings after the war, functioned in part, as a psychological vehicle to contain the highly disruptive experiences of mourning. Adler described the psychological impact of Baeck's experience in Theresienstadt:

> It had bent him and thrown him into mourning, yet it did not break him, because he kept himself ready and open to fresh tasks in a spirit of tenacity and courage. He saw himself as a witness to the existence of another world beyond this fatal 'ghetto.'
>
> *(Adler, 2022 [1955], p. 215)*

Baeck also lost four sisters in Theresienstadt (Meyer, 2021, p. 161), and many friends (e.g., members of his community) which must have been a terrible blow to his everyday existence, including officiating at makeshift funerals. In a word, Baeck had lost his "home world," he had been "thrown" into the death world of Theresienstadt. A home world is "a way of life and a round of activities taken for granted until the point of . . ." incarceration (Goffman, 1961, p. 12).

That is, death anxiety must have pervaded Baeck's everyday existence as the Nazis created a situation where there was an "omnipresent fear of extinction which threatened to run destructively rampant when not successfully kept under safe control by our conviction of the positive value of life" (Bettelheim, 1979, p. 8). Whether in the concentration camp or ghetto, where death anxiety was at its most extreme because these values and social structure were radically assaulted, it is only for example through "autonomy, self-respect, inner integration, a rich inner life, and the ability to relate to others in meaningful ways" that one could "remain human" in the camps, as much as overall conditions and luck would allow (Bettelheim, 1979, p. 109). In Bettelheim's view, the best antidote to the problem of death anxiety is an autonomous and integrated personality that includes a system of beliefs and values which help provide perspective, meaning and coherence to the individual and a social structure that protects a person from abandonment and collapse (Bettelheim, 1979, pp. 10–11). Man, in other words, needs to have a rich, involving, personal and social existence, a meaningful world if he is to sustain himself against death anxiety.

For Bettelheim, and for Baeck, this primarily meant an everyday life of love and work that was saturated with meaning. For Baeck, this love and work was expressed in pastoral responsibilities to his fellow inmates. As Adler (2022 [1955]) noted, Baeck displayed a "willingness to help others" and he was the "conscience of the camp" (p. 215).

According to Bettelheim, the Nazis aimed to completely destroy the inmate's world, eradicating his entire,

> social existence by depriving one of all previous support systems such as family, friends, position in life, while at the same time subjecting one to utter terrorization and degradation through the severest mistreatment and the omnipresent, inescapable, immediate threat to one's very life.
>
> *(Bettelheim, 1979, p. 25)*

In Theresienstadt, this mainly referred to deadly disease, extreme hunger, the threat of deportation onwards, and Nazi sadism and murder (e.g., public hangings). To be incarcerated in Theresienstadt, "meant to be cut off from many aspects of one's previous life. The SS and Nazi state made it amply clear that the life the person had been living was ended; they denied one's former life all validity, now and forever" (Bettelheim, 1979, p. 131).

In the ghetto of Theresienstadt, Baeck and even more so others (as he was a "privileged" inmate) had lost the "delicate web of symbolic identifications available to men and women in normal times" which provides perhaps, most of what we think we are (Des Pres, 1977, p. 214). This is a way of referencing the extreme situation described earlier.

In part, as a way of fending off aforementioned aspects of ghetto life that sought to undermine his autonomy, integration and humanity, Baeck engaged in writing *This People Israel*. Said Baeck:

> This book was written during dark times. In the days when the annihilation of Jewish life had been announced and was being actively pursued, the writer felt impelled to render an account of this Jewish life, this Jewish people.
>
> *(Baeck, 1964 [1955], p. 3)*

Indeed, the focus of *This People Israel* was, according to the jacket cover, to write an,

> existential history of the Jewish spirit, treated as both continuous and progressive revelation of God to history and a deepening and enrichment of the covenant which history and the Jewish people have made with God.
>
> *(Baeck, 1964 [1955])*

In other words, Baeck wrote a history of the Jewish people from biblical times up until the then present, its main purpose being to describe the,

> Jewish spirit in all of its paradoxical complexity: mystery and commandment, law and poetry, individual and community, settled land and desert, uniqueness and universality. Baeck's exegesis of the Book of Moses reveals the faithfulness, the asceticism, the hope, the wisdom of Jewish existence, but also its temptations and failures.
>
> *(Baeck, 1964 [1955])*

One may surmise, that as part of Baeck's mourning process, he concretized his beliefs and values and those of Judaism's in words. We know from his writings and interviews that he believed that it was mainly through action, deeds of goodness, that one instantiates one's beliefs and values, so writing this book was probably part of his praiseworthy deeds, that is, putting his beliefs and values into concrete form and action that could be shared by others.

In my view, Baeck writing this book, partly in Theresienstadt and then after his liberation and the end of the war, was a creative conscious and unconscious way of engaging in a mourning process. That is, Baeck may have written this book while grieving for a vanished, or at least vanishing Jewish world of pre-Nazi Germany, for the members of his flock who had perished, and, more personally, as a way of grieving for his wife who had died six years earlier from the time he was incarcerated in 1943. Said Baeck, "This book should speak before men and bear witness" (1964 [1955], p. 3). The book was "Dedicated to the life and memory of my wife."[6]

He had not seen his daughter, son-in-law and granddaughter for about six years, they had escaped to London after *Kristallnacht*.

As Aberbach (1989) noted, sometimes the ideas of a philosopher may be creatively related to the person's search for meaning and order in the face of loss. John Bowlby, the famous psychiatrist and psychoanalyst who wrote the foreword to Aberbach's book put the matter succinctly:

> Creative writing . . . can attempt many things – to express feelings that are almost inexpressible, to understand what is almost unintelligible, to accept what is at the limit of the bearable, or to restore in symbolic form what cannot be restored in another way. Even in its expression of despair creative writing expresses a search for a way forward.
>
> *(Bowlby, 1989, p. xvii)*

Indeed, it would appear that Baeck's use of writing *This People Israel* was a response to the horror of his situation, the creative act itself being a sign of health and courage, and may have contributed to him being able to press forward while in Theresienstadt. That is, Baeck found a creative way of "mastering" at least partially, the worst aspects of his ordeal of suffering. This is an incredible accomplishment, sublimation, for a man who had difficulty expressing his emotions.

Conclusion

Like other German Jewish theorists, for example, Hermann Cohen, Baeck was focused on the reassertion of Judaism as a religious faith to modern society. His concern was with the universal aspects of Judaism, its ethical ideals, its principles of faith, and the nature of the Jewish mission (Noveck, 1963b). In a word, Baeck stressed the psychological in his approach towards Judaism, he emphasized the unique importance of ethics, that is goodness in Judaism, and focused on furthering the dialogue between Judaism and Christianity (Noveck, 1963c). The prominent theologian, Eugene B. Borowitz provides an apt critique of Beck's overall intellectual contribution to human thought. For example, he criticizes Baeck for not explaining how religious consciousness and ethical comprehension are entwined with each other:

> Why does inner experience need to be limited in action to what the ethical can allow? Why must the ethical command rest on a mysterious ground? One cannot claim their balance is self-evident or even rational for, in substantial measure, they contradict one another. Philosophically these limits go against the teachings of the intellectual schools which created these concepts.
>
> *(Borowitz, 1983, p. 73)*

Borowitz further asks important questions:

> Just how does Baeck know this [i.e., Baeck's allegation of a unity Judaism envisioned and taught through the ages]. What is the methodology by which he ascertains the essence of Judaism? What are the criteria by which he knows what is unessential and secondary? Why has apparently contradictory material been ignored?
>
> *(Borowitz, 1983, p. 74)*

Despite the aforementioned criticisms, Borowitz however, concludes that "there is lasting greatness to Baeck's thought" (Borowitz, 1983, p. 74). For example,

> Baeck reasserted the right of religion to speak to the heart. . . . While granting the virtues of the Neo-Kantian interpretation of Judaism [i.e., Hermann Cohen], he dared to extend its scope and, in so doing, to make the religious life more substantial. He introduced the notion of personal experience into modern Jewish thought and insisted that personal spirituality were part of the essence of Judaism.
>
> *(Borowitz, 1983, p. 74)*

Thus, while his theorizing on the Jewish people and Halacha have been critically challenged, thanks to Baeck, contemporary Jewish thought embraces the notion of religious consciousness as central to authentic Jewish being-in-the-world (Borowitz, 1983, p. 74). Moreover, Baeck demonstrated that Jews have to embrace their suffering ("the grandeur of its suffering" (Baeck, 1964 1955], p. 297)) for their tradition and heritage in order to acquire the right to possess it (Brann, 1963). That is, it was extremely important to Baeck that he communicate his philosophy via the example of his life. Enacting goodness was central to his philosophy.

Notes

1 I have liberally drawn from Meyer's (1999) paper in this section and secondarily, his excellent biography of Baeck (Meyer, 2021).
2 This being said, in a rather unkind manner considering the evidence, Hájková (2020) described Baeck as a "weathered functionary" (p. 54).
3 Baeck might not have described himself as a deliverer of a message from God because it would go against his extreme humility (Meyer, 2024).
4 This statement resonates with Emil Fackenheim's 614th commandment: not to hand Hitler posthumous victories. Jews must survive as Jews.
5 In fact, as is well-known, Buddhist thought rejects the ego or self as a concrete reality to be enhanced and strengthened (Borowitz, 1983). The ego or self is an illusion that one should not cling to.
6 Apparently Baeck had difficulty writing "about personal things" months after his wife had died (Baker, 1978, p. 215).

5

IMPLICATIONS FOR PSYCHOANALYSIS

Baeck was not only a religious believer, he was also a deeply spiritual man. He defines spiritual as "the power of the good, the faculty of religious action" (Baeck, 1948, p. 185). The spiritual life is thus a process through which "a free agent breaks the bonds of external controls and establishes the seat of power within his inner personality" (Lichtenstein, 1963, p. 288). By nearly all accounts this is what Baeck was, for the most part, able to personally accomplish while living in Nazi Germany and in Theresienstadt. This was done both consciously and unconsciously, aspects of his way of being-in-the-world, of his goodness.

In many ways Baeck personified the power of the good in his outlook and behavior. For example, the fact pattern of his challenging life depicts a man with saint-like qualities of mind and heart (Brann, 1963; Kaufmann, 1981a [1958]; Rhée & Dowdey, 2007). Baeck remained in Germany despite being given numerous opportunities to leave his flock and save his own skin; As late as 1939, he brought a trainload of German-Jewish children to England, and then returned to Germany endangering his own life; he served as leader to the German Jewish community outside and inside (to some extent) of Theresienstadt with courage, decency and optimism, despite having to make some very difficult, controversial moral decisions. Regardless of what one thinks of his decisions, there can be no doubt regarding his good intentions and integrity; Baeck did not derive personal benefits from being in a position of some influence in Theresienstadt; he gave lectures from memory on Plato, Kant, Spinoza and Maimónides and others, to his physically and psychologically traumatized fellow inmates giving them some reprieve from their suffering; He supported and comforted his fellow inmates, Jews and non-Jews, with many small acts of human kindness; He was a model for inmates of what it meant to "remain human" in Theresienstadt despite the oppression from their captors; Indeed, philosopher Esther Seidel's statement appears to

DOI: 10.4324/9781003534327-5

be accurate: Baeck exemplifies how a person, when confronted with evil, death and suffering can behave with dignity and self-respect and yet continue to be fully responsible for, and to, his fellow inmates (Seidel, 1995). That is, Baeck's "life and work are a living testimony to resistance of the soul and intellect, a spark that was not extinguished even in Theresienstadt" (Friedlander, 1995, p. ix). The aforementioned is a compelling instance by one extraordinary man of "spiritual resistance." Spiritual resistance as defined by the U.S. Holocaust Memorial Museum website is: "Attempts by individuals to maintain their humanity, personal integrity, dignity and sense of civilization in the face of Nazi attempts to dehumanize and degrade them."

What follows are ten ways Baeck's manner of being-in-the-world, his life and work, can reasonably be applied to psychoanalytic theory and practice. My emphasis is on those valuative attachments that both express and potentiate autonomy, integration and humanity, and are a fertile breeding ground for the cultivation of goodness.

1 The Need For Humanizing Transcendent Beliefs and Values

Extrapolating from the previous discussion of the outlook and behavior of both believing and non-believing inmates in Nazi concentration camps (and Theresienstadt) to ordinary life, it is reasonable to suggest that to the extent that the analysand can fashion strongly felt, flexibly and creatively applied, transcendent-pointing moral beliefs and values that are primarily other-directed, other-regarding and other-serving, he is most likely to be willing and able to maintain his autonomy, integration and humanity, and thus endure and perhaps even surmount his ordeal of suffering. These transcendent-pointing moral beliefs and values can be rooted in God (as with Baeck, Buber, Marcel, Levinas) or its secular equivalent, but what is important is that they be enacted in concrete behavior that regards responsibility for and to the other as primary, or at least as important as oneself. Moreover, such an existential comportment not only involves being willing and able to be ready, receptive, responsive, and responsible to life and the world, but it simultaneously involves metabolizing the shocks of existence that must be borne to actualize the best one can be. These shocks of existence were a daily phenomenon in Theresienstadt, especially when deportation was a persistent, anxiety-ridden possibility. Having to metabolize these shocks of existence happens in some form to all people even in ordinary circumstances.

In particular, I have suggested that pain, sorrow, conflict, and other forms of suffering are fruitfully viewed in terms of helping the analysand give meaning to his suffering by developing an ethical response to it, one that enacts the aforementioned passionately felt, transcendent-pointing moral beliefs and values that are concerned for the best interests of the other. That is, embracing a social ethics of duty and love rather than a crude eudemonism (Beiser, 2018). Freud in fact, put forth a eudemonist morality in his theory (i.e., happiness is the outcome or the determination of the good). Whether it is my own or the other's suffering, the way to make such suffering "sufferable," at least in general terms, is to perceive it as an ethical/moral problem requiring a self-transcending way of thinking, feeling, and acting. As Baeck noted,

> We should not deny pain and persecutions by sinking ourselves in God and explaining all suffering as deceitful appearances; we must affirm suffering with secure certainty; by turning it into an ethical imperative. Do your duty, and the worst will have to become good for you; all the masters and teachers of Israel agreed upon this.
>
> *(Friedlander, 1968, p. 82)*

2 The Need For Courage

What do these ordinary people who behave in extraordinary ways look like in real life? Who are these people we may wish to emulate, including their beliefs, values and behavior? We analysts, who are lodged in a sensibility that conceives of psychoanalysis as a spiritual discipline (Marcus, 2021), may want to not only embrace, but transmit these values to our analysands. For psychoanalysis is a moral psychology, that is, a value-laden dialogue, and as analysts we need to have the courage to acknowledge our commitment to a moral vision. Drawing from the Holocaust literature, Bettelheim (1990, pp. 19, 297) mentions these "righteous ones," who represent the "hope for humanity" that I believe Baeck would most assuredly characterize, and in fact he instantiates: Father Kolbe, a Polish Catholic priest without family, who, while in Auschwitz, volunteered to die in place of a Polish political prisoner, enabling him to survive and return to his wife and children; Janusz Korczak, who steadfastly refused many offers to be saved from extermination in the death camps in order to stay with the orphaned children under his care until they were all murdered by the Nazis; and Miep Gies, a Dutch citizen who, at great personal risk, provided Anne Frank and her family, and the others who hid with them, with the necessary food and supplies that kept them alive, and with the human companionship they required to endure their terrible isolation and ordeal of suffering.

What shines through from the stories of the "righteous ones" is that they epitomized what many would view as a praiseworthy form of life, one characterized by radical autonomy, integration and humanity. Such an art of living (including dying) reflected their commitment to a transcendent-pointing morality as they conceived it, experienced as akin to a categorical imperative—being other-directed, other-regarding and other-serving—as their motivating life principle. That is, such behavior was freely directed at the other's welfare, "it is uncalculated, natural, spontaneous and mostly unreflected-upon manifestation of humanity" (Bauman, 2008, p. 105). While Father Kolbe may have felt an inner command or Voice rooted in his faith in God, and Korczak and Gies had their own irrepressible voice of conscience and responsibility, the fact is that for these extraordinary people their moral actions were enacted for the other's best interests, with no (or little) stake in self-aggrandizement or psychological profit. In my view, while not perfect, for example, he could show "rage and scorn" (Adler, 2022),[1] Baeck may be added to the list of righteous ones.

Of course, from a psychoanalytic point of view, their extraordinary moral behavior was congruent with their "core" transcendent-pointing beliefs and values (roughly their ego-ideal) and thus enhanced their integrity and self-respect, and therefore avoided the toxic feeling that they had not lived up to their moral ideals, a conclusion that probably would have made living with themselves intolerable. These are secondary considerations compared to their main motivation, which was to be for the other before themselves. Their courageous and decent actions did not serve any other purpose, had no ulterior motive (at least for the most part), except to do good (Bauman, 2008). At the same time, their lives reflected an aesthetic outlook, a style of life (even for those in captivity), in which creativity and imagination, practical wisdom and striving towards personal excellence, especially moral excellence, were what mattered most (Kekes, 2002).

3 The Need For Hope

For Marcel, hope is a courageous, though humble affirmation, for it upsurges when one is in captivity, whether it is the captivity associated with, for example, a life-threatening illness, the inevitability of death, intractable depression and/or anxiety or, in Baeck's case, imprisonment. Hope is not merely wishing for a way out of the aforementioned, but goes a step further; to hope, "to trust is to carry within me the personal assurance that however black things may seem, my present intolerable situation cannot be final; there has to be some way out" (Marcel, 2001 [1951], p. 160). For example, to some extent, the person, like the camp or ghetto inmate who affirms that justice will ultimately prevail in the world, be he a believer (e.g., Baeck or a Christian) or a non-believer (e.g., a Marxist or political Zionist), "proclaims that this world *shall come* into existence," and personifies the "prophetic nature of hope" (Marcel, 2001 [1951], p. 159). In other words, while such hoping may seem like auto-suggestion or a self-fulfilling prophecy (and indeed, it sometimes has positive effects in terms of outcome, such as it does in illness), Marcel is suggesting something additional about the experience of hoping itself, namely, that unlike the closedness of auto-suggestion and the self-fulfilling prophecy (which is a "desire" often rooted in fear that aims for a particular outcome, like becoming well or being liberated), it is open to something "more," "higher" and "better" that is hard to pin down. As Marcel says, paradoxically, "the less life is experienced as a captivity the less the soul will be able to see the shining of that veiled, mysterious light, which we feel sure, without any analysis, illumines the very centre of hope's dwelling place" (2001 [1951], p. 32). The analysand too, needs to have a sense of Marcelian hope as he confronts and works through his demons and the like, with or without God.

In the latter context, as Eddington and Shuman (2024) point out, hope is often viewed in terms of the analysand moving closer to what they desire. That is, hope includes the perception that an analysand's goals can be reached. Goals are desired states or actions. Emotions are the consequence of goal pursuits, such that higher levels of hope connect to more optimal patterns of emotion. As the pioneering, positive psychologist Charles Snyder and others noted, hope "is a positive motivational set that is based on the interactively derived sense of successful 1) agency (goal directed energy) and 2) pathways (planning to meet goals)" (Snyder, Rand, & Sigmon, 2018). Eddington and Shuman (2024) further indicated, the correlation "between pathways and agency thinking is that during goal pursuit, pathways thinking enhances agency thinking which leads to increased pathways thinking" (p. 98). In the therapeutic context, such hope often relates to goal-directed behavior. Goals are the "mental targets" that potentiate action sequences, that lead to greater self-esteem, self-continuity and self-coherence. From this perspective, analytic insight is viewed as a strategy that is roughly equivalent to pathways to the analysand's goal of achieving say greater personal adaptation (Eddington and Shuman, 2024, p. 100).

Baeck also had a robust hope structure that was, in part, based on his conviction that "the task of life, in essence" was "that which God has set before man to do" (1964 [1955], p. 195). That is, "one cannot act in truth without suffering" (p. 43), a conviction that was lodged in his deep and abiding faith in God. Faith, said Baeck,

> is the fulfillment of man's relation to the covenant; it forms the unity and the steadiness which he gives his life. Man becomes pious when he experiences himself as being of God, and brings himself to God, so that now no part of his life can exist without this one focal point, without this union
>
> *(Baeck, 1964 [1955], p. 24).*

Indeed, Baeck 's faith embodied his hope structure conceived as a spiritual asset. He noted that "the individual gains his power from the spiritual, out of the fundamental realm in which will, feeling, and thinking are a unity or become one" (1964 [1955], p. 277). Spirit says Baeck, is precisely this aptitude to bind together, to join, to reconcile, to facilitate peace (1964 [1955], p. 210). As Friedlander noted, "All of the squalor and pain, all of the degradation and suffering," in Theresienstadt "could not extinguish the divine spark" in Baeck because the "timeless Word of God was also there; and it was the ultimate reality" (Friedlander, 1964 [1955], p. xx). This divine spark can be conceptualized as a manifestation of Baeck's deep and abiding hope structure. Put differently, "Hope is here a commandment" to be lovingly and fearlessly obeyed (Baeck, 1964 [1955], p. 50).

4 The Need for Patience and Vision

Baeck made the crucial claim that imagination and patience were critical to remaining human in Theresienstadt but also, I believe, while living in the concentration camp society with its oppressive controls. As noted earlier, Baeck defined patience as "this power of resilience that did not let the will to live give way" and imagination as "the vision that ever again and in spite of everything makes him see a future" (Baker, 1978, p. 295). In *This People Israel: The Meaning of Jewish Existence*, Baeck further explicates the dynamic relation between patience and vision:

> Within this people [the Jewish people], two forces were able to unite which are seldom found together: patience and vision. Only where they are found together and permeate one another do they become an historical force. Patience alone could bring man to the point where his soul surrenders, where he yields to everything existing, where every pressure finds him giving way inwardly. Vision alone could lead to the point where man's conscience deserts him, where he abandons his daily duties, where he refused to get himself to the task that approaches him.

However, he continues,

> Only when patience and visions have found one another, when they grow together, are the forces born which master time. Only time can hold fast to the past to establish the conception of today, and simultaneously grasps the future in order to provide the present with courage.
>
> *(Baeck, 1964 [1955], pp. 150–151)*

It is relatively easy to see why patience and imagination are so crucial to the analysand's quest to reduce his personal suffering. For patience enhances decision-making, it permits individuals to reflect on all available options and thus to make well-conceived decisions, rather than acting on impulse or by being swayed by unwieldy emotions. As a result of this, patience can help an individual from being overwhelmed by challenging or hard-going situations, permitting them to manage such situations by allowing time to reflect on what is happening. Most importantly, patience implies that one has a deep and abiding faith that what is "meant" for you will come to fruition in time. Patience involves a will and an ability to be still, it requires trust, and how to discern that which is external to one's life. By cultivating patience, we not only become more tolerant but also learn to accept things as they are and see the larger picture. Patience is like a seed that, when nurtured, flourishes in healthy relationships, positive results, and life-satisfaction.

Vision is defined in the dictionary as the act or power of anticipating which will or may come to be, it gives direction and a glimpse over our life to make our goals and purpose become a reality. In order to understand where we want ourselves to be in life, we must have a clear vision of the totality of our circumstances. Enacting one's vision requires a degree of courage, which significantly increases the chances of succeeding in reaching one's goals. Without vision, one is more likely than not, to succumb to the obstacles and set-backs that constitute living an everyday life, let alone a creative one. Thus, when patience and vision are working together, an analysand is more willing and able to press on despite the challenges.

5 The Need to Creatively Reside Amidst Paradox

Living paradox is dictionary-defined as a rhythmical changing of understandings, the awareness of which emanates from experiencing the contradiction of opposites in the everyday relating of value priorities while journeying to the not-yet. In this view, paradox is a door to hidden truths of life.

Psychoanalysis often equates living paradox with the will and ability to live with ambivalence. Ambivalence is psychoanalytically defined as "the state of having simultaneous contradictory feelings toward an object" (i.e., a person). Moreover,

> ambivalence is always present but may become a clinical issue if one of the feelings are intolerable and repressed. If this occurs, the threat of the repressed feeling coming to awareness may generate anxiety or mobilize defenses that affect functioning.
>
> *(Person et al., 2005, p. 547)*

For Baeck, in Theresienstadt, living paradox involved residing in the "gray zone." As Primo Levi described it, the majority of inmates, for the majority of the time, had to behave amidst a realm of moral and psychological half-tints, which emanates from regimes anchored in terror and servitude (Levi, 1986, p. 58). The capacity to tolerate paradox, in Baeck's system this referred to, for example, three paradoxes: Man's awareness of his human finitude and his infinite strivings; His dependency upon God and the independence of ethical action; and living a life of incalculable worth which is found wanting before God's judgement (Friedlander, 1968). The religious person ideally lives with these paradoxes in a creative tension (Baeck, 1966 [1947]). Put differently, while Freud and his entourage have almost always understood ambivalence to be operative in neurotic human functioning, what Baeck adds to the picture for example, is that ambivalence or paradox has an ontological status, it is intrinsic to the human condition as he construes it. This includes an element of diabolical irony as in Nazi Germany (Cohen, 2014). Helping the analysand to live with ambivalence and paradox that is ultimately unresolvable, with resignation but without despair, becomes one of the goals of a successful analysis. Indeed, much of life is "an eternally unresolved stand-off" (Franks, 2007, p. 67).

6 The Need for Self-Respect

Self-respect is dictionary-defined as a feeling of confidence and pride that one is behaving with honor and dignity. As Baeck noted, in Theresienstadt he engaged in an "ongoing struggle to remain, at least in his own eyes, more than a number, never to capitulate to the filthy surroundings, and always to safeguard his self-respect"

(Meyer, 2021, p. 148). Thus, sustaining his self-respect, including his self-efficacy and self-confidence, was critical to maintaining his autonomy, integration and humanity. Without a robust sense of self-respect, the enactment of goodness is not possible.

Self-respect has many positive functions in an analysand's life, just as a lack of self-respect is utterly destructive to one's self-esteem. As Sanjana Gupta noted (2022), there are at least four benefits of cultivating a robust sense of self-respect.

Individuals who respect themselves comprehend that they must initially look internally to discover their worth, esteem, and happiness. As a consequence, their life tends to be more stable and satisfying than those who rely on external sources of validation.

Individuals with self-respect have a set of beliefs and values by which they judge their character and actions. They have the will and ability to bet all they have on maintaining these norms of behavior, as their very worth and sense of self rely on it. Like a soldier who has come to the last hill and declares, "From here I will not retreat!"

Self-respect requires the person to have the fortitude and strength to establish limits and fight for them when they are threatened. Respecting oneself enough to stand up for one's beliefs, values and boundaries also helps potentiate the respect of others.

Finally, respecting oneself means having a strong sense of dignity toward one's person and position, and always honoring it. By dignity, I mean in part, feeling deserving of respect and honor. As Des Pres (1976) noted, "Dignity . . . appears as a self-conscious, self-determining faculty whose function is to insist upon the recognition of itself *as such*" (p. 73).

Thus, following Baeck, the analysand must understand that self-respect can be conceptualized as the foundation of all goodness. Abraham Joshua Heschel has been attributed with the following: "Self-respect is the root of discipline: The sense of dignity grows with the ability to say no to oneself." This is what we analysts mean by self-overcoming and self-mastery. Moreover, if you have respect for your own beliefs and values, you will quite likely evoke respect from others.

7 The Need for Engaged-Disengagement

I noted in an earlier chapter, Baeck never once used the word 'I,' nor spoke in the first person in his preaching and writing, suggesting that he had a greatly reduced narcissism. I also noted that Baeck was relatively untouched by Theresienstadt. "He never was really there," ghetto inmates observed. That is, he was not touched by the hostile ghetto environment, but he was present for others. Another dialectical paradox, detachment fosters attachment.

"Engaged-disengagement," is especially helpful when one is faced with a world that is bearing down on you. To realize this capacity in real-life, to be able "to be there, but not there," implies that one does not have strong narcissistic strivings that make such creative detachment impossible. For example, one is not so wrapped up in one's own psychological situation that there is no "headspace" for the other. In this context, disengagement is viewed as adaptive behavior, bringing about a degree of greater self-esteem and peace of mind, while engaged in other types of social roles.

There are numerous modern practices that have a family resemblance to engaged-disengagement, such as the non-attachment and the non-self that Taoist and Buddhists beautifully describe, or dynamic immobility in strategic military thinking. And of course, there are those defenses of splitting, denial, compartmentalization and the like, that at their best can point to the value of engaged-disengagement in certain circumstances. Indeed, like Baeck who managed to protect himself from the very worst horrors of Theresienstadt, there is a form of non-egoistic alertness that allows a person to engage, for example, his neurotic suffering while at the same time detach himself from it, while being willing and able to be for the other. While engaged-disengagement may mean appearing to be aloof (one accusation leveled at Baeck), in certain circumstances such a way of being-in-the-world is desirable and worth cultivating. Engaged-disengagement can help potentiate the instantiation of goodness.

8 The Need for Freedom of Thought

Baeck appears to have had the will and ability to maintain his "inner freedom" while living in Nazi Germany and later when incarcerated in Theresienstadt. He largely accomplished this freedom of thought by residing in a different realm of the spirit, in religious feeling, that is, the longing for transcendence and the sense of incomparable dependence on God (Kluback, 1989). It was, in part, through this religious feeling that he maintained the rudiments of his autonomy (i.e., decision-making), integration (i.e., internal harmony) and humanity, relatively speaking.

As the great German-Jewish philosopher Hermann Cohen noted, "If you wish to know what man is, then get to know his suffering," and how he deals with it (Kluback, 1989, p. 130). This book has in part attempted to convey to the reader the nature of Baeck's profound suffering, filtered through his religious symbolic world (e.g., his moral self-consciousness), while living under Nazi oppression and enduring time in Theresienstadt.

Another way of framing Baeck's aforementioned psychological accomplishments is to use the notion of "ego-strength." Ego-strength refers to the capacity to navigate between the demands of the external world (i.e., "reality") on the one hand, and instinctual urges (e.g., sexual and aggressive) and super-ego dictates on the other (e.g., guilt and shame) (Akhtar, 2009). Indeed, inferring from Baeck's biography he appears to have had the qualities of a "healthy" individual: For example, he had good self-object differentiation, a lack of neurotic defensive functioning, an effective modulation of his drives and affects, and sound reality testing (Person et al., 2005), even in the oppressively surreal world of the ghetto. An individual like Baeck, with a strong ego, is thus, one who is able to endure frustration and stress, delay gratification, change selfish desires when required, and resolve internal conflicts and emotional problems before they are catalyzed into neurosis or some other subverting condition. All of this is in sync with one of the important goals of psychoanalysis as Freud noted: "Analysis does not set out to make pathological reactions impossible, but to give the patient's ego *freedom* to decide one way or another" (Freud, 1923, p. 50).

What I have tried to suggest in this book is the importance of the analysand developing the capacity to make conscious thoughtful decisions (hopefully good ones). For example, as Holocaust survivor Viktor Frankl (1963) has indicated, between a stimulus and a response there is a headspace. That is, in that headspace resides the power to choose one's response, and it is through this response that our psychological growth and freedom reside. In other words, freedom is what you do with what has been done to you.

Psychoanalysis is, of course, aware of the importance of inner freedom from neurosis and the like, especially when it comes to implementing reasonable consequential thinking. However, what should be in sharp focus is the need for the analysand to develop the capacity for wise decision making, in part based on the observation that, following Herbert Marcuse (1964), the span of choice open to the person is not the crucial element in determining the degree of human freedom, but what can be chosen and what is chosen by the person.

This being said, as Freud suggested, the majority of people do not really desire freedom, mainly because freedom involves responsibility, and the majority of people are fearful of it. Thus, there is a wide range of defense mechanisms which are designed to circumvent freedom including self-deception, and other, more subtle attempts to avoid truth and to keep it concealed from oneself (i.e., bad faith), and the like. This can also involve those analysands who obsess about decisions, feeling that there is a perfect answer to the problem before them. They lack the freedom to make decisions because of their fear of being wrong in their black and white world. To overcome this tendency requires a degree of self-confidence about what one thinks and the ability to tolerate an imperfect solution. This is what Baeck had to face when making a number of impossible and fateful decisions.

9 The Need to Strive for Holiness (or goodness)

Striving for holiness is not a typical psychoanalytic notion or category, but it has the potential to be useful, for it broadens the goal of any successful analysis and puts into sharp focus the human aspiration for "something more," "something higher" and "something better." An authentic spirituality in a largely secular world. There are, "vibrant possibilities of religious language for revealing unanticipated dimensions of our intersubjective lives" (Oppenheim, 2017, p. 71).

That is, along with health, adaptation and the like, there can be holiness as a goal, a straightforward way of addressing Freud's concerns: As mentioned in the introductory chapter, in the letters to American neurologist James Jackson Putnam,

Freud wrote "That psychoanalysis has not made analysts themselves better, nobler, or of stronger character remains a disappointment for me. Perhaps I was wrong to expect it" (Hale, 1971, pp. 163–164). The aforementioned is in harmony with Freud's overall outlook on the human condition, "The unworthiness of human beings, including the analyst, always impressed me deeply, but why should analyzed men and women in fact be better. Analysis makes for integration but does not itself make for goodness" (Hale, 1971, p. 188).

Implicit to Baeck's life and scholarship is the overarching goal of achieving holiness, which, as with Levinas, is more of a direction one pursues than an endpoint. While Baeck does not formally define the term, it is an implicit core concept in his lived life and writings. Baeck, like Levinas, relates holiness to ethics. What is important to be mindful of is that for Baeck, ethics is lodged in the mysterious grounding in God (Borowitz, 1983) and the main thrust of holiness is a way of being-in-the-world that is other-directed, other-regarding and other-serving, especially other-serving, for example, as demonstrated in Baeck's kindhearted and helpful outlook and behavior inside and beyond Theresienstadt. As Baeck notes, "All men proceed towards the same holy goal. . . . Moral assertion of the self, the full awareness of equality, the messianic certainty of God's kingdom" (Friedlander, 1968, p. 79). Holiness then, was the forward thrust of the Divine power, an upward, ceaseless impetus toward "something more," something higher" and "something better", for example, as instantiated by a striving for moral perfection (Agus, 1963). Levinas puts this point aptly: "The concern for the other breaches concern for the self. That is what I call holiness. Our humanity consists in being able to recognize the priority of the other" (Levinas, 2001, p. 234).

Perhaps it is time to bring the notion of holiness into psychoanalysis (e.g., the spirit of holiness, ethical spirit (Cohen, 2014)) and making it the ultimate affect-integrating, meaning-giving and action guiding hermeneutic horizon. Such a version of the self or subjectivity can expand and deepen what an analysand is capable of at their best.

10 The Need for Resistance

Said Baeck, "The greatness of the human soul is its power of resistance" (Gruenewald, 1957, p. 195). "Moral strength rises out of moral resistance" (Baeck, 1964 [1955], p. 45).[2] I believe that these quotations aptly depict Baeck's existential orientation while enduring Nazi oppression. Indeed, Baeck sounds rather similar to Michel Foucault, the great French theorist of power-relations. Foucault said that there is not something outside of power-relations, but rather, it is a potentiality internal within it. Resistance, understood as agonistic struggle and strategic interaction, is itself a form of power. While power is omnipresent, as it was amidst the Nazi assault, it is inseparable from challenge and struggle: "where there is power, there is resistance" (Foucault, 1990, p. 95). Elsewhere he notes, "that aside from torture and execution, which preclude any resistance, no matter how terrifying a given system may be, [and Theresienstadt was terrifying] there always remain the possibilities of resistance, disobedience, and oppositional groupings" (Foucault, 1980, p.138). In other words, embedded in the power relationship and "constantly provoking it, are the recalcitrance of the will and the intransience of freedom" (Foucault, 1994, p. 12).

In my view, Baeck frequently resided in the "headspace," enacting what Goffman described as "an essential constituent element of the self," that is, the individual is a "stance taking entity (Goffman, 1961, pp. 319–320). In a certain sense, wretched and appalling as Theresienstadt was, Baeck was willing and able to use his strongly felt ethico-religious resources in order not to be terrorized by death. That is, he was able to fend off, at least to some degree, toxic forces that were designed to subvert his autonomy, integration and humanity. Goodness, expressed in many ways, was his antidote to the Nazi onslaught.

Thankfully, most of us have not been incarcerated in a concentration camp or ghetto, but I believe Baeck's devotion to an attitude of resistance has some bearing on the typical analysand. That is, we live a "liquid life" (Bauman, 2005) one of instability, uncertainty and unsafety, in part rooted in the boundless growth of technology ("the accelerated pace of change in the social setting" (Bauman, 2005, p. 116), with which personality integration cannot keep up:

> Liquid life is a precarious life, lived under conditions of constant uncertainty. The most acute and stubborn worries that haunt such a life are the fears of being caught napping, of failing to catch up with fast-moving events, of being left behind, of overlooking 'use by' dates, of being saddled with possessions that are no longer desirable, of missing the moment that calls for a change of tack before crossing the point of no return.

Moreover, he continues,

> Liquid life is a succession of new beginnings – yet precisely for that reason it is the swift and painless endings, without which new beginnings would be unthinkable that tend to be its most challenging moments and most upsetting headaches . . . liquid life is consuming life.
>
> *(Bauman, 2005, pp. 2, 9)*

How does one protect oneself from the worst aspects of a liquid life?

Given the fact that many of the fundamental structures that society is organized around are melting away, that is, life is liquid, to some extent one has to be willing and able to "go with the flow," "learning to walk on quicksand" as Bauman aptly describes it (2005, p. 116). This requires great technical skills, for example, situational awareness and the ability to adapt to the unfixed nature of everyday life. This necessitates lifelong education that constitutes the art of living that promotes reasonable choice, says Bauman.

However, one can best achieve integration of the personality if one has embraced the beliefs and value-laden attachments that Baeck and others have lived by, such as courage, hope and being-for-the-other and so forth. In the words of the prophet Micah, "do justice, love mercy, and walk humbly with your God." That is, one must have an inner center of gravity, that acts as an affect-integrating, meaning-giving, action-guiding force in one's personality. If situations, ideas, and plans are fluid, if they are not fixed and are likely to change, often repeatedly and unexpectedly, but if one has a set of heart-felt, humanizing personal beliefs, values and essential convictions, one can make better decisions in everyday life, and thereby maintain the rudiments of autonomy, integration and humanity. Thus, Martin Buber and Gabriel Marcel believe that something like a "spiritual core" is the deepest center of the person (perhaps calling to mind Winnicott's "sacred core of the personality, the incommunicado self" (Hoffman, 2011, p. 144), Eigen's "living center" or "spiritual center" (Eigen, 1998, pp. 15, 58, 125) and Loewald's "ego core" (1962, p. 498)). It is in this domain that there resides a guiding principle in the fluid world and which provides the basis for the possibility of an openness to the transcendental dimension, and the goodness that it demands. It is here that the person experiences what one may characterize as ultimate reality. This includes the discovery of that core, the dynamics of its development, and its journey to the ultimate goal, however defined. Indeed, all this has been magnificently detailed by the great religions and spiritual movements of the world.

Final Word: The Need for a Psychoanalytic Social Psychology

Baeck's observations of his fellow inmates in Theresienstadt are in sync with those of survivors of concentration and death camps, namely, that these extreme environments brought out the best and the worst behavior in inmates. There were the kind and helpful inmates in Theresienstadt, as described by Adler on the one hand, and on the other, those who were only out for themselves and were willing and able to survive at any price.

Such an observation puts into sharp focus the fact that psychoanalysis has not developed a sophisticated social psychology that can better account for behavior in an extreme situation. That is, to better comprehend how radically unstable social environments like the ghettos and camps impacted personality change and functioning. In other words, better understanding when personality and social context are in interaction, when both of them are changing (Bettelheim, 1960).

As one prominent analyst, Martin S. Bergmann, noted "we have a very rudimentary social psychology as psychoanalysts" (in Luel & Marcus, 1984, p. 216). More recently, Greenberg noted, "within mainstream psychoanalysis, there has been relatively little emphasis on 'real events,' including the effects of adult-onset trauma," such as illness in old age, or in our case, surviving a Nazi ghetto or camp or some similar oppressive setting (Greenberg, 2016, p. 43). While the notion of "reality" is a very complex one, "By 'reality,' psychoanalysis means what is *actually out there*, can be objectively perceived and consensually agreed upon" (Akhtar, 2009, p. 240). However, experimental/scientific social psychology experiments, such as Asch's line judgement studies (highlighting conformity versus independence), Milgram's obedience to authority experiments (highlighting obedience versus resistance), Latané and Darley's bystander studies (highlighting helping versus indifference in emergencies), or Zimbardo's Stanford Prison Experiment (highlighting tyranny versus autonomy), showed how perception is reality (Marcus, 2020). As the holistic practitioner Asher Prasad noted, "This means when you have an idea of something, and your brain is convinced of the truth, then it is the truth. It becomes the truth" (Prasad, 2024, n.p.). In a word, comprehension follows perception.

Of course, many eminent psychoanalytic personality and social theorists have investigated the role of culture on the individual, such as the way that one socially constructs a self within the context of family and the broadly conceived environment (e.g., the role of gender, patriarchy, race, economics, etc.). While these theorists have tried to delineate the ways that individuals are shaped by macro social circumstances, including acknowledging social context as being a primary determinant of behavior, intra-psychic properties (e.g., desire and fantasy) tend to dominate the analysis of why people behave the way they do.

While much good work has been done by these theorists, they are incomplete. What psychoanalysis has not done, which I believed is a huge deficit in psychoanalytic theory and practice, is to develop a sophisticated psychology of everyday "situational" behavior that gives robust consideration to specific contextual factors in determining behavior on vitally important moral issues.

Such moral issues include for example, "Why do we conform and obey?" "Why do we oppress?" "Why do we help and support?" (Haslam & Smith, 2017, p. 2). A sophisticated social psychology does this by providing scientific analysis of the relationship between "mind and society" that sometimes challenges mainstream psychoanalytic thinking (Haslam & Smith, 2017, p. 1). That is, social psychology concentrates on scientifically explaining and understanding people engaging in "real" behavior in "real situations." This real life micro experimental/scientific methodology is in sync with those who have argued for an "evidence-based" psychoanalysis that focuses on the "here and now" and therapeutic immediacy between analyst and analysand (Luyten et al., 2015).

What would a psychoanalysis look like if it incorporated the aforementioned perspective and findings into its theory and practice? If the typical analysand embraced the perspective and findings of experimental/scientific social psychology, it would for example, lead to a greater "situational awareness." That is, an increased awareness of one's surroundings (e.g., of time and space) and identifying potential threats and dangerous situations, is a mind-set and ego strength that has enormous benefits in helping the analysand maintain personal and collective security. Put differently, analysands would become aware of the diverse ways the external world impacts and shapes their outlook and behavior, including their moral compass. In fact, most people most of the time are unconscious of how the micro external world effects their outlook and behavior.

As I have tried to show throughout this book, Baeck had the will and ability to be largely immune from the toxicity of the Theresienstadt environment, and hence, he was able to maintain his moral compass in the face of dehumanization and the like. He was both "there and not there," that is, he was able to be there for his suffering fellow inmates, an expression of goodness, but not there for the worst aspects of the ghetto environment. Such a "divided self," the positive basis of Baeck's identity formation, acted something like a psychological "protective cocoon" or "sacred canopy" amidst the extreme conditions of Theresienstadt.

Notes

1 An alternative interpretation of Baeck's rage and scorn has been noted by Meyer (2024). "Does the moral person not rage and scorn when encountering that which damages the human image?"

2 Susannah Heschel (2021) recently characterized Baeck as exemplifying "prudent resistance against the Nazis."

REFERENCES

Aberbach, D. (1989). *Surviving Trauma: Loss, Literature and Psychoanalysis*. New Haven, CT: Yale University Press.

Adler, H.G. (2022 [1955]). *Theresienstadt 1941–1945: The Face of a Coerced Community*. Cambridge: Cambridge University Press.

Agus, J. (1963). Abraham Isaac Kuk. In S. Noveck (Ed.), *Great Jewish Thinkers of the Twentieth Century* (pp. 72–96). New York: B'nai B'rith Department of Adult Education.

Akhtar, S. (2009). *Comprehensive Dictionary of Psychoanalysis*. London: Karnac Books.

Améry, J. (1980). *At the Mind's Limits: Contemplations by a Survivor on Auschwitz and its Realities* (Trans. A. Rosenfeld & S. P. Rosenfeld). Bloomington, IN: Indiana University Press.

Angress, R.K. (1985). *Simon Wiesenthal Center Annual, Vol. 2*. New York: Kraus International Publications.

Baeck, L. (1947). Why Jews in the World? A Reaffirmation of Faith in Israel's Destiny. *Commentary*, 3, 501–507.

Baeck, L. (1948). *The Essence of Judaism*. (Trans. I. Howe). New York: Schocken Books.

Baeck, L. (1957). Excerpts from Baeck's Writings. *Leo Baeck Institute Year Book*, 2(1), 35–47.

Baeck, L. (1958). *God and Man in Judaism*. New York: Union of American Hebrew Congregations.

Baeck, L. (1964 [1955]). *This People Israel: The Meaning of Jewish Existence* (Trans. A. H. Friedlander). Philadelphia, PA: Jewish Publication Society of America.

Baeck, L. (1966) [1947]. *The Pharisees and Other Essays*. New York: Schocken Books.

Baeck, L. (1981a [1958]). *Judaism and Christianity: Essays by Leo Baeck* (Trans. W. Kaufmann). New York: Antheum.

Baeck, L. (1981b). Does Traditional Judaism Possess Dogmas? In A. Jospe (Ed.), *Studies in Jewish Thought: An Anthology of German-Jewish Scholarship* (pp. 41–53). Detroit, MI: Wayne State University Press.

Baeck, L. (2022 [1955]). Foreword. In H.G. Adler, *Theresienstadt 1941–1945. The Face of A Coerced Community* (Trans. B. Cooper) (p. xi). Cambridge: Cambridge University Press.

Baker, L. (1978). *Days of Sorrow and Pain: Leo Baeck and the Berlin Jews*. New York: Macmillan Publishing Company, Inc.

Bamberger, F. (1958). *Leo Baeck: The Man and the Idea. The Leo Baeck Memorial Lecture 1* (pp. 1–15). New York: Leo Baeck Institute.

Bauman, Z. (1989). *Modernity and the Holocaust*. Ithaca, NY: Cornell University Press.

Bauman, Z. (2005). *Liquid Life*. Cambridge: Polity Press.

Bauman, Z. (2008). *The Art of Life*. Cambridge: Polity Press.

Beiser, F. C. (2018). *Hermann Cohen: An Intellectual Biography*. Oxford: Oxford University Press.

Bellah, R. N., Madsen, R. Sullivan, W. M., Swidler, A., & Tipton, S. M. (1986). *Habits of the Heart: Individualism and Commitment in American Life*. New York: Harper & Row.

Berg, J. M., Grant, A. G. & Johnson, V. (2010). When Callings are Calling: Crafting Work and Leisure in Pursuit of Unanswered Occupational Callings. *Organization Science, 21*(5), 973–994.

Berger, P. L. (1967). *The Sacred Canopy: Elements of a Sociological Theory of Religion*. Garden City, NY: Doubleday.

Berger, P. L. & Berger, B. (1972). *Sociology: A Biographical Approach*. New York: Basic Books.

Berkovits, E. (1979). *With God in Hell*. New York: Sanhedrin Press.

Bernstein, R. (2002). Evil and the Temptation of Theodicy. In R. Bernasconi & S. Critchley (Eds.), *The Cambridge Companion to Levinas*. Cambridge: Cambridge University Press, pp. 252–267.

Bettelheim, B. (1960). *The Informed Heart: Autonomy in the Mass Age*. Glencoe, IL: The Free Press.

Bettelheim, B. (1979). *Surviving and Other Essays*. New York: Knopf.

Bettelheim, B. (1990). *Freud's Vienna and Other Essays*. New York: Knopf.

Binswanger, L. (1963). *Being in the World*. (Trans. J. Needleman). New York: Basic Books.

Bondy, R. (1980). The Theresienstadt Ghetto: Its Characteristics and Perspective. In Y. Gutman & A. Saf (Eds.), *The Nazi Concentration Camps: Structure and Aims, The Image of the Prisoner, The Jews in the Camps*. Proceedings of the Fourth Yad Vashem International Historical Conference (pp. 303–314). Jerusalem: Yad Vashem.

Borowitz, E. B. (1983). *Choices in Modern Jewish Thought: A Partisan Guide*. New York: Behrman House.

Bowlby, J. (1989). Foreword. In D. Aberbach, *Surviving Trauma: Loss, Literature and Psychoanalysis* (pp. vi–viii). New Haven, CT: Yale University Press.

Brann, H. W. (1963). Leo Baeck. In S. Noveck (Ed.), *Great Jewish Thinkers of the Twentieth Century* (pp. 133–157). New York: B'nai B'rith Department of Adult Education.

Busch, T. W. (Ed.) (1987). *The Participant Perspective: A Gabriel Marcel Reader*. Lanham, MD: University Press of America.

Cain, S. (1979). *Gabriel Marcel*. South Bend, IN: Regnery/Gateway.

Cain, S. (1995). *Gabriel Marcel's Theory of Religious Experience*. New York: Peter Lang.

Chasseguet-Smirgel, J. (1985). *Creativity and Perversion*. New York: W. W. Norton & Company.

Cohen, H. (1971). *Reason & Hope. Selections from the Jewish Writings of Hermann Cohen*. (Trans. & Ed. Eva Jospe). Cincinnati, OH: Hebrew Union College Press.

Cohen, H, (2014). *Spinoza on State & Religion Judaism & Christianity* (Trans. R.S. Schine). Jerusalem: Shalem Press.

Des Pres, T. (1976). *The Survivor: Anatomy of Life in the Death Camps*. New York: Pocket Books.

Dwork, D. (1991). *Children with a Star*. New Haven, CT: Yale University Press.

Early, T., & Gallagher, K. T. (2003). Marcel, Gabriel. In B. L. Marthaler (Ed.), *New Catholic Encyclopedia, Vol. 9* (2nd ed.) (pp. 133–135). Detroit, MI: Thomson Gale/The Catholic University of America.

Eddington, N. & Shuman, R. (2024). Positive Psychology II. *Continuing Psychology Education*, 86–106. Albany, New York.

Eigen, M. (1998). *The Psychoanalytic Mystic*. Binghamton, NY: ESF Publishers.

Elliach, Y. (1980). Jewish Tradition in the Life of the Concentration Camp Inmate. In Y. Gutman & A. Saf (Eds.), *The Nazi Concentration Camps: Proceedings of the Fourth Yad Vashem, International Historical Conference* (pp. 195–206). Jerusalem: Yad Vashem.

Fackenheim, E. L. (2001). After Auschwitz, Jerusalem: In Memory of My Teacher, Leo Baeck. *Judaism*, 50(1), 53–59.

Feller, Y. (2024). *The Jewish Imperial Imagination: Leo Baeck and German-Jewish Thought*. Cambridge: Cambridge University Press.

Foucault, M. (1980). Power and Strategies. In C. Gordon (Trans. & Ed.), *Power/Knowledge: Selected Interviews and Other Writings, 1972–1977* (pp. 134–145). Brighton: Harvester Press.

Foucault, M. (1989). The Ethics of the Concern for Self as a Practice of Freedom. In S. Lotringer (Ed.), *Foucault Live: Collected Interviews, 1961–1984* (pp. 432–449). New York: Semiotexte.

Foucault, M. (1990). *The History of Sexuality, An Introduction, Vol. 1*, New York: Vantage Books.

Foucault, M. (1994). The Ethic of Care for the Self as a Practice of Freedom (Trans. J. D. Gauthier). In J. Bernhauer & D. Rasmussen (Eds.), *The Final Foucault* (pp. 1–20). Cambridge, MA: MIT Press.

Frankl, V. E. (1963). *Mans's Search for Meaning*. New York: Pocket Books.

Franks, P. W. (2007). Jewish Philosophy after Kant: The Legacy of Salomon Maimon. In M. L. Morgan, & P. E. Gordon (Eds.), *Modern Jewish Philosophy* (pp. 52–79). Cambridge: Cambridge University Press

Freud, S. (1927). Post-script to a Discussion of Lay Analysis. In J. Strachey (Trans. & Ed.). *Standard Edition of the Complete Psychological Works of Sigmund Freud, Vol. 20*. (pp. 251–258). London: The Hogarth Press.

Freud, S. (1923). The Ego and the Id. In J. Strachey (Trans. & Ed.). Standard Edition of the Complete Psychological Works of Sigmund Freud, Vol. 19 (pp. 3–66). London: The Hogarth Press.

Friedlander, A.H. (1964 [1955]). Introduction. In L. Baeck, *This People Israel: The Meaning of Jewish Existence* (Trans. A. H. Friedlander) (pp. ix–xxii). Philadelphia, PA: Jewish Publication Society of America.

Friedlander, A. H. (1968). *Leo Baeck: Teacher of Theresienstadt*. New York: Holt, Rinehart, & Winston.

Friedlander, A.H. (1995). Foreword. In W. Homolka, *Jewish Identity in Modern Times. Leo Baeck and German Protestantism* (pp. ix–xiv). Oxford: Berghahn Books.

Friedlander, A. H. (2024). Leo Baeck. *Encyclopedia Britannica*, https://www.britannica.com/biography/Leo-Baeck. Accessed October 25, 2024.

Friedman, M. (1963). Martin Buber. In S. Noveck (Ed.), *Great Jewish Thinkers of the Twentieth Century* (pp. 183–209). New York: B'nai B'rith Department of Adult Education.

Fromm, E. (1947). *Man for Himself: An Inquiry into the Psychology of Ethics*. New York: Henry Holt.

Fromm, E. (1968). *The Revolution of Hope: Toward a Humanized Technology*. New York: Harper and Row.

Fromm, E. (1973). *The Anatomy of Destructiveness*. New York: Holt, Rinehart and Winston.

Fryer, D. R. (2004). *The Intervention of the Other: Ethical Subjectivity in Levinas and Lacan*. New York: Other Press.

Gallagher, K. (1962). *The Philosophy of Gabriel Marcel*. New York: Fordham University Press.

Geertz, C. (1973). *The Interpretation of Culture*. New York: Basic Books.

Giddens, A. (1991). *Modernity and Self-Identity*. Stanford, CA: Stanford University Press.

Godfrey, J. J. (1987). Appraising Marcel on Hope. *Philosophy Today*, *31*(3), 234–240.

Goffman, E. (1961). *Asylums*. New York: Anchor Books.

Greenberg, T. M. (2016). *Psychodynamic Perspectives on Aging and Illness* (2nd ed.). Dordrecht/Heidelberg/London/New York: Springer.

Grobman, A. (1983). Attempts at Resistance in the Camps. In A. Grobman & D. Landes (Eds.), *Genocide: Critical Issues of the Holocaust* (pp. 243–255).Chappaqua, NY: Russell Books.

Gruenewald, M. (1957). Leo Baeck: Witness and Judge. *Judaism*, *6*(3), 195–201.

Gupta, S. (2022). The Impact of Self-Respect on Your Life. *VeryWellMind*. https://www.verywellmind.com/self-respect-importance-influences-and-strategies-for-improvement-6823525. Accessed October 25, 2024.

Hadot, P. (1997). *Philosophy as a Way of Life*. Oxford: Blackwell Publishing.

Hájková, A. (2020). *The Last Ghetto: An Everyday History of Theresienstadt*. Oxford: Oxford University Press.

Hale, N. G. (Ed.). (1971). *James Jackson Putnam and Psychoanalysis* (Trans. J. B. Heller). [Letter from Freud to Putnam, November 13, 1913, pp. 163–164; Letter to Putnam, June 17, 1915, p. 188]. Cambridge: Cambridge University Press.

Haslam, S. A. & Smith, J. R. (2017). An Introduction to Classic Studies in Social Psychology. In J. R. Smith & S. A. Haslam (Eds.), *Social Psychology: Revisiting the Classic Studies* (2nd ed.) (pp. 1–10). Los Angeles, CA: Sage Publications.

Healy, M. J. (2023). Hope and Despair in Marcel: Images and Underlying Attitudes. *Marcel Studies*, *8*(1), 35–44.

Heschel, S. (2021). The Essence of Dignity [Book Review: Michael A. Meyer, *Rabbi Leo Baeck: Living a Religious Imperative in Troubled Times*]. *Jewish Review of Books*, Summer 2021. https://jewishreviewofbooks.com/holocaust/11104/the-essence-of-dignity/. Accessed October 25, 2024.

Hoffman, M. T. (2011). *Towards Mutual Recognition: Relational Psychoanalysis and the Christian Narrative*. London: Routledge.

Homolka, W. (1995). *Jewish Identity in Modern Times: Leo Baeck and German Protestantism*. Oxford: Berghahn Books.

Huberband, S., Gurock, J. S. & Hirt, R. S. (1987). *Kiddush Hashem: Jewish Religious and Cultural Life in Poland During the Holocaust*. Hoboken, NJ: KTAV Publishing House.

Jones, J. W. (1991). *Contemporary Psychoanalysis & Religion*. New Haven, CT: Yale University Press.

Katz, C. E. (2014). *An Introduction to Modern Jewish Philosophy*. London: I.B. Tauris.

Kaufmann, W. (Trans.) (1981a [1958]). Biographical Introduction. In *Judaism and Christianity: Essays by Leo Baeck* (pp. 3–19). New York: Antheum.

Kekes, J. (2002). *The Art of Life*. Ithaca, NY: Cornell University Press.

Keen, S. (1967). *Gabriel Marcel*. Richmond, VA: John Knox Press.

Kluback, W. (1989). *The Legacy of Hermann Cohen*. Atlanta, GA: Scholars Press.

Laing, R. D. (1962). Ontological Insecurity. In H. M. Ruitenbeck (Ed.), *Psychoanalysis and Existential Philosophy* (pp. 41–54). New York: E. P. Dutton & Company.

Landes, D. (1983a). Spiritual Responses in the Camps. In A. Grobman & D. Lanes (Eds.), *Genocide: Critical Issues of the Holocaust* (pp. 261–278). Chappaqua, NY: Russell Books.

Landes, D. (1983b). Spiritual Responses in the Ghettos. In A. Grobman & D. Lanes (Eds.), *Genocide: Critical Issues of the Holocaust* (pp. 196–211). Chappaqua, NY: Russell Books.

Langer, L. L. (1982). *Versions of Survival*. Albany, NY: State University of New York Press.

Levi, P. (1986). *The Drowned and the Saved*. New York: Summit Books.

Levinas, E. (1969). *Totality and Infinity: An Essay on Exteriority*. (Trans. A. Lingis). Pittsburgh, PA: Duquesne University Press.

Levinas, E. (1981). *Otherwise than Being or Beyond Essence* (Trans. A. Lingis). Dordrecht/Boston/London: Kluwer Academic Press.

Levinas, E. (1985). *Ethics and Infinity* (Trans. R. A. Cohen). Pittsburg, PA: Duquesne University Press.

Levinas, E. (1989). *Difficult Freedom: Essays on Judaism*. (Ed. Sean Hand). Baltimore, MD: Johns Hopkins University Press.

Levinas, E. (1998). *Entre Nous: Essays on Thinking-of-the-Other* (Trans. M. B. Smith & B. Z. Harsnav). New York: Columbia University Press.

Levinas, E. (2001). *Is it Righteous to Be? Interviews with Emmanuel Levinas*. (Ed. J. Robbins). Stanford, CA: Stanford University Press.

Lichtenstein, A. (1963). Joseph Soloveitchik. In S. Noveck (Ed.), *Great Jewish Thinkers of the Twentieth Century* (pp. 281–297). New York: B'nai B'rith Department of Adult Education.

Loewald, H. W. (1962). Internalization, separation, mourning and the super-ego. *Psychoanalytic Quarterly*, 31(4), 83–504.

Luel, S. A. & Marcus, P. (Eds.) (1984). *Psychoanalytic Reflections on the Holocaust: Selected Essays*. New York: University of Denver and KTAV Publishing House.

Luyten, P., Meyers, L. C., Fonagy, P., Target., M., & Blatt., S. J. (Eds.). (2015). *Handbook of Psychodynamic Approaches to Psychopathology*. New York: Guilford Press.

Lynch, W. F. (1965). *Images of Hope*. New York: Mentor-Omega Books.

McGuire, W. (Ed.). (1974). *The Freud/Jung Letters*. Princeton, NJ: Princeton University Press.

Marcel, G. (1965). *Being and Having: An Existentialist Diary* (Trans. K. Farrer). New York: Harper and Row.

Marcel, G. (1973). *Tragic Wisdom and Beyond* (Trans. S. Jolin and P. McCormick). Evanston, IL: Northwestern University Press.

Marcel, G. (1995). *The Philosophy of Existentialism* (Trans. M. Harari). New York: Carol Publishing Group.

Marcel, G. (2001 [1951]). *The Mystery of Being: Faith and Reality, Vol. 2*. South Bend, IN: St. Augustine's Press.

Marcus, P. (1999). *Autonomy in the Extreme Situation: Bruno Bettelheim, the Nazi Concentration Camps and the Mass Society*. Westport, CT: Praeger.

Marcus, P. (2008). *Being for the Other: Emmanuel Levinas, Ethical Living and Psychoanalysis*. Milwaukee, WI: Marquette University Press.

Marcus, P. (2013). *In Search of the Spiritual: Gabriel Marcel, Psychoanalysis and the Sacred*. London: Karnac Books.

Marcus, P. (2017). *The Psychoanalysis of Career Choice, Job Performance, and Satisfaction: How to Flourish in the Workplace*. London: Routledge.

Marcus, P. (2020). *Psychoanalysis, Classic Social Psychology and Moral Living*. London: Routledge.

Marcus, P. (2021). *Psychoanalysis as a Spiritual Discipline: In Dialogue with Martin Buber and Gabriel Marcel.* London: Routledge.

Marcus, P. (2023). *Psychoanalysis and Toileting: Minding One's Business.* London: Routledge.

Marcus, P. (2024). *Psychoanalysis and Wisdom: Encountering 'Ethics of the Fathers'* London: Routledge.

Marcuse, H. (1964). *One Dimensional Man.* Boston, MA: Beacon Press.

Meyer, M. A. (1999). The Thought of Leo Baeck: A Religious Philosophy for a Time of Adversity. *Modern Judaism, 19*(2), 107–117.

Meyer, M. A. (2021). *Rabbi Leo Baeck: Living a Religious Imperative in Troubled Times.* Philadelphia, PA: University of Pennsylvania Press.

Meyer, M. A. (2024). Personal communication, 19 June 2024.

Montefiore, L. G. (1958). Foreword. In L. Baeck, *God and Man in Judaism* (pp. 7–8). New York: Union of American Hebrew Congregations.

Montes, A. (2023). Gabriel Marcel and Dietrich von Hildebrand on Freedom: Fidelity and Hope as Necessary for Freedom. *Marcel Studies*, 8(1), 21–34.

New World Encyclopedia (2022). Leo Baeck. *New World Encyclopedia.* https://www.newworldencyclopedia.org/p/index.php?title=Leo_Baeck&oldid=1083856. Accessed October 25, 2024.

New World Encyclopedia (2024). Gabriel Marcel. *New World Encyclopedia.* https://www.newworldencyclopedia.org/p/index.php?title=Gabriel_Marcel&oldid=1141737. Accessed October 25, 2024.

Noveck, S. (1963a). Ahad Ha-am. In S. Noveck (Ed.), *Great Jewish Thinkers of the Twentieth Century* (pp. 11–44). New York: B'nai B'rith Department of Adult Education.

Noveck, S. (1963b). Editor's Introduction. In S. Noveck (Ed.), *Great Jewish Thinkers of the Twentieth Century* (pp. 3–9). New York: B'nai B'rith Department of Adult Education.

Noveck, S. (1963c). Editor's Introduction. In S. Noveck (Ed.), *Great Jewish Thinkers of the Twentieth Century* (pp. 99–104). New York: B'nai B'rith Department of Adult Education.

Oppenheim, M. (2017). *Contemporary Psychoanalysis and Modern Jewish Philosophy.* London: Routledge.

Ornstein, A. (1985). Survival and Recovery. *Psychoanalytic Inquiry*, 5(1), 99–130.

Pawelczyńska, A. (1979). *Values and Violence in Auschwitz: A Sociological Analysis* (Trans. C. S. Leach). Berkeley, CA: University of California Press.

Pax, C. (1975). Marcel's Way of Creative Fidelity. *Philosophy Today*, 1(25), 12–21.

Person, E. S., Cooper, A. M., & Gabbard, G. O. (2005). *Textbook of Psychoanalysis.* Washington, D.C., American Psychiatric Publishing.

Pingel, F. (1991). The Destruction of Human Identity in the Concentration Camps: The Contribution of the Social Sciences to the Analysis of Behavior under Extreme Situations. *Holocaust and Genocide Studies*, 6(2), 167–184.

Prasad, A. (2024). Why Perception is Reality and How to Control It. *Dr. Asha.* https://drashaprasad.com/personal-development/perception-reality/. Accessed October 25, 2024.

Pruyser, P. W. (1963). Phenomenology of dynamics of hoping. *Journal for the Scientific Study of Religion*, 3(1), 86–96.

Rabinowicz, R. A. (Ed.), (1982). *Passover Haggadah: The Feast of Freedom* (2nd ed.). New York: Rabbinical Assembly.

Rheé, R., & Dowdey, D. (Trans.). (2007). *Dialogues with Leo Baeck.* New York: iUniverse, Inc.

Rokeach, M. (1968). Attitudes. In D. L. Sills (Ed.), *International Encyclopedia of the Social Sciences, Vol. 1* (pp. 450–454). New York: Macmillan Company and The Free Press.

Rorty, R. (1989). *Contingency, Irony and Solidarity.* Cambridge: Cambridge University Press.

Rorty, R. (1991). *Objectivity, Relativism, and Truth.* Cambridge: Cambridge University Press.

Rosthal, R. (1964). Translator's Introduction. In G. Marcel, *Creative Fidelity* (Trans. R. Rosthal). (pp. iv–xxvi). New York: Farrar, Straus and Giroux.

Sacks, J. (2024a). Shabbat Announcements, Great Neck Synagogue, March 16, 2024, 1–2.

Sacks, J. (2024b). Shabbat Announcements, Great Neck Synagogue, October 5, 2024, 1–2.

Schafer, R. (1976). *A New Language for Psychoanalysis.* New Haven, CT: Yale University Press.

Schrag, C. O. (2000). Gabriel Marcel. In J. K. Roth (Ed.), *World Philosophers and Their Words, Vol. 2.* Pasadena, CA: Salem Press.

Schweid, E. (1994). Prophetic Mysticism in Twentieth Century Jewish Thought. *Modern Judaism*, 4(2), 139–174.

Seidel, E. (1995). Epilogue. In W. Homolka, *Jewish Identity in Modern Times: Leo Baeck and German Protestantism* (pp. 110–125). Providence, RI: Berghahn Books.

Seligman, P. (1967). Review of *This People Israel. The Jewish Quarterly Review*, 57(3), 242–246.

Simon, A. (2024). Leo Baeck. In Judaism, Biographies. *Encyclopedia.com.* https://www.encyclopedia.com/people/philosophy-and-religion/judaism-biographies/leo-baeck. Accessed October 25, 2024.

Snyder, C. R., Rand, K. L., & Sigmon, D. R. (2018). Hope Theory: A Member of the Positive Psychology Family. In M. W. Gallagher & S. J. Lopez (Eds.), *The Oxford Handbook of Hope* (pp. 27–44). New York: Oxford University Press.

Stratton-Lake, P. (1998). Marcel on Hope. In Hope. *Routledge Encyclopedia of Philosophy.* https://www.rep.routledge.com/articles/thematic/hope/v-1/sections/marcel-on-hope. Accessed October 25, 2024.

Todorov, T. (1996). *Facing the Extreme: Moral Life in the Concentration Camps.* New York: Metropolitan Books.

U. S. Holocaust Memorial Museum (2024) Theresienstadt, Holocaust Encyclopedia, https://encyclopedia.ushmm.org/content/en/article/theresienstadt. Accessed October 25, 2024.

Weinstein, F. (1980). *The Dynamics of Nazism.* New York: Academic Press.

Wertheimer, J. (1987). Leo Baeck. In Judaism, Biographies. *Encyclopedia.com.* https://www.encyclopedia.com/people/philosophy-and-religion/judaism-biographies/leo-baeck. Accessed October 25, 2024.

Wiesel, E. (1974). Talking, and Writing and Keeping Silent. In F. H. Littell & H. G. Locke (Eds.), *The German Church Struggle and the Holocaust* (pp. 269–277). Bloomington, IN: Wayne State University Press.

Williams, B. (1993). *Ethics and the Limits of Philosophy.* London: Routledge.

Winnicott, D. W. (1971). *Playing and Reality.* London: Tavistock Publications.

Wolf, A. J. (2004). Heschel's 'Torah from Heaven.' *Judaism*, 53(3–4), 300–309.

Wuthnow, R. (2024). Rediscovering the Sacred: Perspectives on Religion in Contemporary Society. *Religion Online.* https://www.religion-online.org/book-chapter/chapter-1-sacredness-a. Accessed October 25, 2024.

Wyschogrod, E. (1988). Concentration Camps and the End of the Life-World. In A. Rosenberg & G. E. Meyers (Eds.), *Echoes from the Holocaust: Philosophical Reflections on a Dark Time* (p. 338). Philadelphia, PA: Temple University Press.

INDEX

Note: Page numbers followed by "n" denote endnotes.

Aberbach, D. 78
Absolute Thou *see* God
Adler, H. G. 14, 41, 92; on Baeck 40, 44, 48, 56, 75, 76; on kindhearted people 44; on Theresienstadt 42, 46, 47, 50–51, 65n13; typology of inmates 47, 65n5, 67, 92
agency 22, 44, 47, 49, 60, 84; *see also* pathways
ambivalence 86
Améry, J. 2, 14, 19, 44, 46, 51–52, 53, 61, 63, 64
antisemitism 22, 23, 75
Arendt, H. 28
art of living 2, 8, 82, 91
Auschwitz 14, 19, 26, 27, 42, 43, 44, 51–52, 53, 56, 63, 82; *see also* concentration and death camps; inmates/prisoners
autonomy 2, 4, 12–16, 20, 22, 41–51, 61–64, 76, 81
availability 34

Baeck, N. 5, 24
Baker, L. 7, 9n4, 18–19, 22, 24, 26, 35, 47, 51, 57, 65n15, 75
Bauman, Z. 43; liquid life 91
belief: defined 14; transcendent 2, 81–82
Bellah, R. N. 15, 16
Berger, P. 61–63
Bergmann, M. S. 92
Berkovits, E. 54, 61, 64
Bettelheim, B. 13–14, 43, 61, 64; antidote to death anxiety 76; autonomy for 13; concentration camp experiences/observation 19–20, 41, 42, 44, 45, 46, 48–50; essential convictions 48; extreme situation 15; as Holocaust survivor 2, 9n6; inmates complying with authority 49; integration for 13; remaining human for 14, 41, 44; righteous ones for 82; splitting 51
Binswanger, L. 4
B'nai B'rith 5, 24
Bondy, R. 42
Borowitz, E. B. 21, 72, 74, 75, 78–79
Bowlby, J. 78
Brann, H. W. 9n10, 10n17
Broch, H. 42
Buber, M. 3, 9n6, 11n28; religiosity against religion 9n11; spiritual core 92
Buber-Neumann, M. 57
Buddhism 73; as a religion of egotism 73

Cain, S. 36
calling 15, 16; *see also* work
career 15–16
Chasseguet-Smirgel, J. 2
Children with a Star (Dwork) 42
choiceless choice 43, 44

Christianity 11n28; Judaism *vs.* 7, 73–75; as a romantic religion 7, 74
Cohen, H. 3, 21, 88; on autonomy 38n3
Cohen, M. 65n14
commandment 4, 7, 13, 16–18, 30, 47, 60, 66–68; *see also* mystery
Communists 57
concentration and death camps: Bettelheim's observation 15, 19–20, 41, 42, 44, 45, 46, 48–50; death anxiety 76; group membership 56–59; society 19, 22, 28, 30; survivors 9n6, 92; *see also* inmates/prisoners; Theresienstadt
courage 33–34, 82–83
creative writing 78
creativity 20
culture 93
Czapski, D. 39n15

Das Wesen des Christentums (Harnack) 7
Day of Atonement *see* Yom Kippur
death anxiety 76
desire 30, 32, 35
despair and depression 34, 35
Des Pres, T. 14, 43, 87
The Destruction of the European Jews (Hilberg) 28
Development of the Legal Position of Jews in Europe, Primarily in Germany from Antiquity to the Beginning of the Age of Enlightenment 23
Dieses Volk: Jüdische Existenz (Baeck) 7; *see also This People Israel: The Meaning of Jewish Existence* (Baeck)
dignity 54–56, 87; *see also* self-respect
Dilthey, W. 4, 7
dogma 11n29
Dwork, D. 42–43
dysentery 11n25

Eddington, N. 84
ego-strength 88–89; defined 88
Eichman in Jerusalem (Arendt) 28
Eigen, M. 92
Einsatzgruppen 26
Emerson, R. W. 23
emotions: being consequence of goal pursuits 84
empathy 7
engaged-disengagement 87–88
The Essence of Judaism (Baeck) 7, 20, 28–29, 67, 73
essential convictions 48
ethical imagination 29
ethical monotheism 7, 21, 66, 72, 73, 74
ethics 68; holiness and 90
eudemonism 81–82
evil: for Baeck 61; for Levinas 60
experimental/scientific social psychology experiments 93
extreme situation: defined 15

Feller, Y. 21, 22, 23, 26, 33, 37, 38n6, 61
First World War 4
Foucault, M. 8, 38n4; power-relations 90–91; resistance 90–91
Frank, A. 65n9, 82
Frankl, V. E. 2, 14, 43, 44, 64, 65n9, 89
freedom: Baeck on 39n14; defense mechanisms 89; Freud on 89; inner 88–89; of thought 88–89
Freud, S.: ambivalence 86; eudemonist morality 81–82; freedom 89; letters to Putnam 1, 89–90
Friedlander, A. 19; on Baeck 3, 11n28, 16, 20, 28, 29, 67, 84; "Mystery and Commandment" 16, 67; on paradoxes central to Baeckian system 20
Fromm, E. 20, 39n18
Fryer, D. R. 2

Gandhi 38n8
Geertz, C. 59, 63–64
Giddens, A. 47, 50
Gies, M. 82
gift: hoping as a 33
goals 84; as mental targets 84
God 4, 13, 20, 21, 61, 62, 66–77, 84; as Absolute Thou 36, 38; ancient Rabbis 53; as enigmatic and ambiguous 52–53; ethics 90; as an external other 63; freedom of thought 88; hope and 36, 83; an intimate presence 52; Jewish existence 54–55; judgement 86; kingdom 90; martyrdom and 53–54, 65n11; mystery and commandment 4, 7, 13, 16–18, 30, 33, 47, 59, 66–68; prayers 24–26, 39n16; religious consciousness (*see* religious consciousness); sacred moral code 60; self and 41; as self-sustaining transcendent truth 59; as self-sustaining universal matrix 4; suffering and 28–29, 34, 52–53, 60; *sukkah* 58; transcendent-pointing moral beliefs and values 81
Goffman, E. 46, 91
Goldstein, K. 33–34

goodness: defined 1
grace 33
gray zone 42
Greenberg, T. M. 92
guilt 50
Gupta, S. 87

Habits of the Heart (Bellah) 15
Hadot, P. 8
Hájková, A. 15, 39n15, 65n6, 65n10, 70–71
Halevi, J. 17
Haltung 55
Harnack, A. V. 7, 74–75
Hasidim 58
headspace 88, 89, 91
Hebrew piety 37
Hebrew Union College 6
Herrmann, J. 1
Herzl, T. 65n14
Heschel, A. J. 3, 9n10, 87
Heschel, S. 1, 94n2
Hess, M. 31
Hilberg, R. 28
Hindu Indians 68
historical patience 30
Hitler, A. 5, 13
Hochschule für die Wissenschaft des Judentums 4, 5
holiness 17, 68; Baeck and 68, 90; striving for 89–90
Holocaust 82; spiritual resistance 12; suffering (*see* suffering); *sukkot* 64; survivors 1, 2, 10n23, 19, 38; theodicies 60–61
home world 75
homiletics 5
Homolka, W. 3
hope/hoping 31–36; authentic 34; auto-suggestion 83; Baeck and 84; as a boundary concept 30; captivity 33; as a centrifugal movement 35; desire *vs.* 35; dispositional 37–38; as an exigency 32; Fromm on 39n18; as a glue 35; goal-directed behavior 84; as a kind of gift 33; need for 83–84; phenomenology 32; self-fulfilling prophecy 83; Snyder on 84; time and 35; willing receptivity and engagement with others 36
humanity 2, 4, 12–17, 20, 29, 44–51, 61–64; defined 14; imagination and patience 30, 84–86; *see also* inmates/prisoners
humiliation 19, 20, 50
humility 17, 34–35

imagination and patience *see* vision
inmates/prisoners 1–2; Adler on 42, 47, 65n5, 67, 92; agency 44; as autonomous individuals 41, 44–45; Bettelheim's observation 19–20, 41, 42, 44, 45, 46, 48–50; central struggle for 44; choiceless choice 43; Christian or Catholic 2; complying with authority 49; death 6; deportation 28; essential convictions 48; extreme situation 15; humiliation 20; lectures/lecturing to 6; Levi's observation 42; massification 41, 47; moral dilemmas 43–44; Pawelczyńska's observation 42; propaganda events by Jewish functionaries 39n13; rationality of 43; religion and 3; religious observances and rituals 57, 58, 62; religious symbols/symbolism 59–60, 62–64; security of being 20; self-esteem 19–20, 45, 54; self-identity 20, 49, 51; self-respect 19, 54–56; splitting 51; suffering 44, 51, 54; Todorov's observation 57; *see also* Judaism
integration 2, 4, 12–16, 20, 45; defined 13–14; personality 91–92; *see also* inmates/prisoners
internalization 63
intra-psychic properties 93
Israel 53–54
Italiener, B. 21

Jehovah's Witnesses 57
Jewish history 71–73
Jews/Jewish people 5, 71–73; apologetic outlook 75; as chosen people 72–73; ethical monotheism 7, 21, 66, 72, 73, 74; proselytization 72; *see also* inmates/prisoners; Judaism
job 15–16
Judaism 4, 21, 23, 66–79; Christianity *vs.* 7, 73–75; as classical religion 7, 74; as communal way of being 21; dialectic polarity 17–18; features 68–69; Harnack on 7; humanity 36; liberal 9n8, 9n11, 61, 62; martyrdom 53–54, 65n11; mystery 33; prayers 24–26, 39n16; prophetic 68–71; as a religion of altruism 73; as a religion of optimism 9–10n12, 30, 37; religious consciousness 66; as a sacred canopy 64; wisdom of 28
Jung, C. 6

Kaufmann, W. 1
Kiddush Hashem 53–54

Kolbe (Father, Catholic priest) 82
Korczak, J. 82
Kristallnacht 5, 18, 19, 78

Laing, R. D. 22–23
Langer, L. 43–44, 58
Levi, P. 2, 14, 42, 44, 64, 86
Levinas, E. 1, 8, 9n6, 90; evil for 60; holiness (or saintliness) for 17; incarceration 65n16; responsibility for 21; suffering for 60; theodicy for 60–61
Lincoln, A. 9n5
liquid life 91
living paradox 86
Loewald, H. W. 92
Luther *vs.* Paul 73, 74

Marcel, G. 9n6; "Being" for 39n22; hope/hoping 31–36, 83; ontological exigence 36; prideful person for 34; "Sketch of a Phenomenology and a Metaphysic of Hope" 36; spiritual core 92
Marcuse, H. 89
martyrdom 53–54, 65n11
massification 41, 47
Meyer, M. A. 19, 79n1; on Baeck 5, 9n5, 10n14, 18, 24, 25–27, 29, 55, 66, 67, 68, 70, 72, 74, 94n1; on Judaism 71; on lecturing in Theresienstadt 8n3; on mass suicide 27; on optimism 39n20; on prayers composed by Baeck 25–26; on prophets 70
Micah (prophet) 92
Midrash 5
mitzvoth (commandments) 68
Montefiore, L. G. 54
mortality saliency 66
mystery 4, 7, 13, 16–18, 33, 66–68; *see also* commandment
"Mystery and Commandment" (Friedlander) 16, 67
mysticism: Baeck and 6, 10n14; prophetic 6

National Representation of Jews in Germany 5, 47, 65n8
Nazis/Nazism: Baeck cooperating with 26, 28, 43; Communists 57; compliance to 48–49; essential convictions 48; goal 41, 47; radical evil of 61, 62; *see also* Baeck, L.; concentration and death camps; inmates/prisoners; Theresienstadt
non-egoistic alertness 88
Nuremberg Laws 24, 25

objectification: defined 63
ontological exigence 36
ontological security 22–23, 47, 50, 58
Ornstein, A. 56–57
orthoprax 16

Pasachoff 22
pathways 84; *see also* agency
patience: authentic hope and 34; decision-making and 85; defined 85; historical 30; vision and 30, 84–86
Paul *vs.* Luther 73, 74
Pawelczyńska, A. 2, 42, 44, 46, 49, 61, 64
Person, E. S. 65n12
piety 37
Pingel, F. 51
polarity 20–21; religion of 4, 17–18, 20
Prasad, A. 93
prayers 24–26, 39n16; Shabbat Nachamu 24–25; Yom Kippur 25–26
Prinz, J. 21
prisoners *see* inmates/prisoners
prophetic mysticism 6
prophets 17, 68–71; Baeck on mind and heart of 69–70; Meyer on 70; religion to 69; strength 70; thoughts of 69; *see also* Judaism
Pruyser, P. W. 30, 32
psychoanalysis 80–94; Chasseguet-Smirgel on 2; conceptualization 7–8; as a discipline 2; Freud on 2; Fryer on 2; as a spiritual discipline 4, 82; as a spiritual exercise 8
Putnam, J. J. 1, 89–90

reality: notion of 92–93; perception as 93
Reichmann, E. 18, 22
Reichsvertretung der Deutschen Juden *see* National Representation of Jews in Germany
religious consciousness 16; Baeck 21, 47, 52, 66, 72; defined 66; ethical comprehension and 78; Jewish 66; *see also* God; inmates/prisoners; Judaism
religious observances and rituals 57, 58, 62
religious symbols/symbolism 59–60, 62–64
resistance 90–92; Foucault on 90–91
reverence 17, 30
righteous ones 82–83

'Romantic Religion' (Baeck) 73–75
Rorty, R. 19, 41, 50
Rosenzweig, F. 3, 11n28, 16, 39n16

Sabbath 22, 24, 38–39n10, 57, 58
Sacks, J. 65n17
The Sacred Canopy (Berger) 62
sanitation 11n25
Scholem, G. 28
Seidel, E. 2, 80–81
self 41–42; for Baeck 41; for Bettelheim 41; defined 41; sense of 15, 42; work and 15–16
self-esteem 15, 41, 42; inmates/prisoners 19–20, 45, 54
self-fulfilling prophecy 83
self-identity 2; Baeck's narrative of 15, 46, 49, 50; Giddens on 47; inmates 20, 49, 51
selfobject 57, 65n12
self-respect 86–87; for Baeck 18, 41, 47; beliefs and values 87; inmates 19, 54–56; loss of 54
self-transcendence 51–54
shocks of existence 81
Shuman, R. 84
Simlai (Rabbi) 4
Simon, A. 18
situational awareness 91, 93–94
"Sketch of a Phenomenology and a Metaphysic of Hope" (Marcel) 36
Snyder, C. 84
social psychology 92–94; experimental/scientific experiments/studies 93
spirit 12
spiritual core 92
spiritual exercises 8
spiritual life 80
spiritual resistance: criticism 38n2; defined 12–13, 81; *see also* inmates/prisoners; Theresienstadt
split consciousness 51
splitting 51
suffering 9n9, 28–29, 60, 79, 80–82, 84, 88; Baeck 9–10n12, 10n22, 30, 33, 46, 48, 50, 51, 52, 72, 78, 88; devout Jews 52–53, 60; as ethical imperative 28; God and 28–29, 52–53; hoping 34; inmates 44, 51, 54; theology of 6
sukkah 58
sukkot 64
symbolic world 53

Talmud 17, 22, 52
theodicy 60–62, 64
Theresienstadt 1941–1945 (Adler) 40
Theresienstadt 4, 5–6, 8n2, 40–64; death anxiety 76; intellectual activity 58–59; as an inverted world 50; liberation of 6; life in 76; Nazi goal in 41, 47; religious observances and rituals 57, 58, 62; religious services 57; religious symbols/symbolism 59–60, 62–64; sanitation in 11n25; self-transcendence 51–54; shocks of existence 81; as a transit camp 42; welfare program 10n21
This People Israel: The Meaning of Jewish Existence (Baeck) 7, 22, 31, 75, 77–78, 85
Tillich, P. 27, 66
Tisha B'Av 24, 39n11
Todorov, T. 14, 44, 57, 64
transcendence 31–32
transcendent beliefs and values 2, 81–82, 83

U.S. Holocaust Memorial Museum 81

value: defined 14; demonic collapse or decay of 42; transcendent 2, 81–82
vision: courage 85; defined 85; patience and 30, 84–86
Vorlesungen über das Wesen des Judentums see The Essence of Judaism (Baeck)

Weimar Republic 75
Wiesel, E. 2, 14, 19, 44, 46, 61, 64, 65n7
Winnicott, D. W. 20, 92
work 15–16; as a calling 16; job and career orientation 15–16
World Union for Progressive Judaism 6
Wuthnow, R. 62, 63
Wyschogrod, E. 44

Yitzhak, L. 52
Yom Kippur 5, 24, 25; prayer 25–26

Zionism 7, 23, 65n14
Zuruckhaltung 55